Macdonald illustrated war studies

German Airborne Troops
British Airborne Troops
Carrier Fighters
Hitler's Elite – *Leibstandarte SS*

Forthcoming
The U.S. Strategic Bomber
The E-Boat Threat
The U-Boat Hunters
The World War II Bomber

WORLD WAR II FIGHTER CONFLICT

WORLD WAR II
FIGHTER CONFLICT
Alfred Price

Macdonald and Jane's: London

First published in 1975
by Macdonald and Jane's
(Macdonald & Co. (Publishers) Ltd)
Paulton House, 8 Shepherdess Walk
London N1 7LW

Typesetting, Bedford Typesetters Ltd
Made and Printed in Great Britain by
Morrison & Gibb Ltd
London and Edinburgh

ISBN 0 356 08129 X

Layout and make-up: Michael Jarvis
Drawings and diagrams: Peter Endsleigh Castle ARAeS

Contents

Wing Commander
R. R. Stanford-Tuck
DSO, DFC.

Foreword.
by Wing Commander R R Stanford-Tuck DSO DFC

I had just finished reading the manuscript of *World War II Fighter Conflict* and was concentrating my thoughts before putting pen to paper, when a news broadcast arrested my attention: 'Air Chief Marshal Sir Keith Park, who commanded No 11 Group of Fighter Command during the Battle of Britain, has died in New Zealand at the age of eighty-two . . .'

My mind flashed back to those roaring days in 1940 when I had served under him. I had a vivid mental picture of him in his white flying helmet lobbing in at our airfield in his Hurricane, to get at first hand our impressions of the battle in which he was playing such a leading role.

In June 1940 I was ordered to Farnborough with George Stainforth (who had taken the world air speed record in 1931 in a Supermarine S6B floatplane). We were to carry out one of the first comparative trials, between a Spitfire and the first flyable Messerschmitt 109 obtained by the RAF. After the first 'combat' George and I swapped aircraft and repeated it, to ensure that the results were not distorted by any differences in our respective flying skills. Later, when I found myself in actual combat with 109s, these trials were to prove of inestimable value to me; for I knew exactly my enemy's strengths and his weaknesses.

On the day after the comparative trial was completed I was summoned to see Air Vice Marshal Park, as he then was. He wanted to know everything about it, and fortunately I had taken my rough notes and could give him all the details. This great commander was keenly interested in his machines' capabilities *vis-à-vis* those of the enemy. And that is what this excellent book is all about.

Alfred Price has written a book which, although on a complex and technical subject, is highly readable even to the uninitiated; he has done it in such a manner that I think it will be read by young and old with keen interest. Many years ago, as a fighter leader in the thick of air combat, I would have given a great deal to have had at my fingertips the information contained in this book. I feel sure that *Fighter Conflict* will be received throughout the world with great interest and enthusiasm, and I should like to congratulate Alfred Price on giving us such a comprehensive and well-researched work.

Bob Stanford Tuck.

Sandwich Bay 7th February 1975

Introduction.

My aim in putting together this book has been to show, in general terms, how the fighter aircraft and its tactics evolved during the Second World War. To cover such a wide field within the confines of a book of this size, I have had to stick closely to the 'kernel' of the fighter genre, the day fighter. I have omitted any reference to fighter-bombers or specialised night fighter aircraft, which may be the subject of later books in this series. Furthermore, I have restricted the coverage to those fighter aircraft and weapons which actually saw service during the Second World War, or which would have seen service had the war continued a little longer. To enable the reader 'to see the wood instead of the trees', I have made no attempt to describe in detail every type of fighter which saw service; nor have I tried to mention every tactical innovation. I have, however, gone to pains to show the general pattern of technical and tactical developments, which bore a remarkable similarity in all of the major combatant nations.

The greatest problem in writing a book of this sort has been to fashion the abundance of material into a shape consistent with reality, to follow the main highway of development and eschew the blind alleys. For this I have been fortunate in being able to draw on assistance from some of the leading experts in their respective fields. On questions of aerodynamics, Sir Morien Morgan CB, MA, FRS, ex-director of the Royal Aircraft Establishment at Farnborough; on structures Mr Percy Walker CBE, PhD, FRAeS, ex-head of the Structures Department at Farnborough; on power plants Mr D. McCarthy BSc, the Chief Engineer Staff Engineering, Rolls-Royce Ltd; and on armament the late Air Marshal Sir Ralph Sorely FRAeS, who was Assistant Chief of Air Staff (Technical Requirements) from 1941 to 1943 and Controller of Research and Development at the Ministry of Aircraft Production from 1943 to 1945. On questions of tactics I was helped by Group Captain Robert Oxspring DFC and two bars, AFC, who flew fighters throughout the Second World War including the Battle of Britain, and continued to do so long afterwards; Colonel Reade Tilley DFC, U.S.A.F., who participated in some of the hardest-fought fighter versus fighter actions of the war in the skies round Malta; and ex-Luftwaffe Leutnant Johann Pichler, Knight's Cross, who fought on the eastern and western fronts and was credited with 75 victories of which sixteen were American heavy bombers. I am deeply grateful for the help I have received from these gentlemen. I must stress, however, that I alone am responsible for the opinions expressed in this book.

In illustrating this book I have drawn on material from many good friends. In particular I should like to thank Hanfried Schliephake, John Taylor, Harry Holmes, J. B. Cynk, Bruce Robertson, Françoise Rude and *Icare* magazine, Chaz Bowyer, Kenneth Munson, Werner Girbig, Jim Oughton and Hans Redemann. And, last but certainly not least, I should like to thank Peter Endsleigh Castle for doing such a magnificent job of the cover and the line drawings.

UPPINGHAM   ALFRED PRICE
RUTLAND

In this book the aircraft weights stated are those for the fighter at take-off in normal fighting trim, that is to say without drop tanks or other external stores. The miles given are statute miles, and speeds are given in statute miles per hour. The weapon calibres given are those usually used with the weapon being described, ie .5-inch Browning machine gun or 20-mm Mauser cannon. Armour thicknesses are given in millimetres.

1 Honing the Blade.

Cannon and fire-arms are cruel and damnable machines;
I believe them to have been the direct suggestion of the Devil.

MARTIN LUTHER

By the beginning of 1934 it was possible to visualise the sort of bomber that would be in service by the end of the decade: the sleek all-metal monoplane with a cruising speed of over 250 mph at altitudes around 20,000 feet, possibly with armour protection for the crew. Scores of such bombers, flying in tight formations for mutual defence, would, it was believed, overwhelm the fighter opposition and lay waste the defenceless cities and industrial areas below. These were the times when Stanley Baldwin's famous dictum 'The bomber will always get through' reigned supreme. In 1934 the best-equipped air forces operated low-powered fabric-covered strut-braced fixed-undercarriage biplane fighters armed with two rifle-calibre machine guns with maximum speeds of just over 200 mph, which took about ten minutes to reach 20,000 feet (in which time the new bombers would cover about 40 miles); they were in every case without effective ground control, and in many cases without even the simplest radio equipment. Clearly a great deal would have to be done before Stanley Baldwin would be proved wrong.

The increasingly unsettled international situation, bringing closer the possibility of large scale air attack, slowly began to loosen the purse-strings which had throttled fighter development during the preceding sixteen years. With time breathing down their necks designers in Great Britain, the U.S.A. and Germany, Italy, France, Russia and Japan began work on a new breed of fighter to counter the bomber of the future. The same advances in aerodynamics, structures and engines that increased the performance of bombers could also be applied to fighters; with these, and similar improvements in air-to-air weapons, it might be possible to redress the balance between the attack and the defence.

The fighter now demanded by the various air forces was, first and foremost, to be a *bomber destroyer*. If there was time to spare and if it was able, it could do battle with its own kind; but the destruction of bombers was to be the primary reason for its being. To get into a firing position on fast high-flying bombers of the type mentioned, the new generation of fighters would require, above all, a high maximum speed and a very good climbing performance. To knock down the tough new bombers when they got within range, they would require the heaviest possible armament they could carry without jeopardising the other two requirements. Manoeuvrability and radius of action had in each case to be adequate, but they were not primary requirements.

Representative of the fighters in service in 1934 was the Hawker Fury biplane operated by the Royal Air Force, depicted here. Powered by a Rolls-Royce Kestrel engine developing 525 horsepower, the Fury had a maximum speed of 207 mph at 14,000 feet. It carried an armament of two .303-inch Vickers guns and had a loaded weight of just under 4,000 pounds. *Haine*

The PZL 11, which made up the backbone of the Polish fighter force, had entered service in 1935 and was obsolete by the summer of 1939 when the Second World War broke out. Powered by a 645 horse-power Bristol Mercury engine built under licence the main production version, the PZL 11c, had a maximum speed of 242 mph at 16,000 feet; it carried an armament of two or four 7.7-mm machine guns and had a loaded weight of only 3,960 pounds. *Cynk*

This, then, was the background to the design of the fighters which entered service just before war broke out in 1939. They were completely different from their 1934 predecessors, both in shape and capability. The new aircraft were for the most part all-metal cantilever monoplanes, with enclosed cockpits, retractable undercarriages, multi-gun armaments, engines developing around 1,000 horse-power and top speeds of well over 300 mph. Backing the new fighters in the air forces of Great Britain and Germany was an aid whose effectiveness, though still unproven, was potentially enormous: the omniscient eye of radar.

With such far-reaching technological jumps in almost all aspects of fighter design during a period of only half a decade, it would be surprising if designers and tacticians had been able to foresee accurately every primary and secondary result of the new developments. And, indeed, they would be proved wrong on some aspects. But with so much change within such a short time it is surprising not that mistakes were made, but that the mistakes were not larger. Such was the excellence of design of some of the fighters which took shape in 1934 that they were, with modifications, still effective fighting machines eleven years later at the end of a war quite different from that originally envisaged by their creators.

The mainstay of the French fighter force in the summer of 1939 was the Morane 406, a machine which was nearing obsolescence. Powered by an 860 horse-power Hispano Suiza 12Y engine, this fighter had a maximum speed of 304 mph at 15,000 feet. Armed with one 20 mm cannon and two 7.5-mm machine guns, it had a loaded weight of 5,360 pounds.
E. C. Armees

The 'State of the Art' in 1939

To observe the results of the fighter designers' frantic endeavours to meet the threat of the new bomber, we shall now examine the best features of five of the most advanced aircraft in service in September 1939: the British Spitfire Mark I, the German Messerschmitt 109E-1, the American P-36C Hawk, the Russian Polikarpov I-16 Type 17 and the finest twin-engined fighter, the German Messerschmitt 110C-1.

At the beginning of the war the Spitfire, in its Mark I version, was just beginning to enter service in quantity in the Royal Air Force. It was a low wing monoplane of conventional layout of all-metal construction. The flying control surfaces, the ailerons, elevators and rudder, were fabric covered. The main undercarriage legs were retractable but the tail wheel was fixed. This fighter was powered by a Rolls-Royce Merlin III liquid-cooled V-12 engine of 27 litres capacity; with a mechanically-driven

single-stage single-speed supercharger it developed a maximum of 1,030 horse-power at 5,500 feet using 87 octane petrol. This power was converted into thrust by a three-bladed two-speed propeller, with a fine blade angle setting for take-off and a coarse setting for use at high speed.

The Spitfire I was armed with eight .303-inch Browning machine guns, mounted in the wings to fire forwards outside the propeller arc. These weapons fired ball, incendiary or armour-piercing rounds each weighing just under an ounce, at a rate of 1,150 per minute per gun, with a muzzle velocity of 2,400 feet per second; the ammunition box for each weapon carried a maximum of 300 rounds. These guns were aimed using a simple fixed-graticule reflector sight. At the beginning of the war the Spitfire carried no armour protection for the pilot, or self-sealing or other protection for the fuel tanks.

The total fuel capacity of 84 Imp (100 U.S.) gallons was housed in two separate tanks mounted one on top of the other, between the rear of the engine and the forward wall of the cockpit. A further unprotected tank of 7.5 Imp (8.9 U.S.) gallon capacity, fitted underneath the engine, housed the oil. These were sufficient to give the Spitfire I an effective operational radius of action of about 160 miles.

The early Spitfires carried a high frequency radar telephone low in clarity and unpredictable in range, to enable the pilot to maintain contact with his comrades and his ground controller.

The early versions of the Mark I Spitfire had a normal loaded weight of about 5,700 pounds, which gave them a wing loading of just under 24 pounds per square foot and a power loading of 5.1 pounds per horse-power. It had a cantilever wing of very thin section, with a thickness/chord ratio of 13 per cent at the root. These factors combined to make the Spitfire a remarkably fast and manoeuvrable aircraft at low and medium levels

Opposite:

One of the best fighters in service in September 1939 was the Supermarine Spitfire; at that time the Royal Air Force had a total of 187 equipping 10½ squadrons. Powered by a Rolls-Royce Merlin III developing 1,030 horse-power, the Mark I had a maximum speed of 362 mph. Armed with eight .303-inch machine guns, it had a loaded weight of 5,700 pounds. The aircraft depicted carried the early two-blade fixed-pitch propeller; by the summer of 1939 Spitfires were being delivered with three-bladed two-pitch propellers. *C. Brown*

The layout of the Spitfire Mk 1

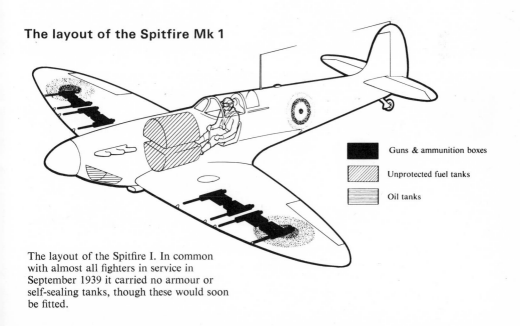

Guns & ammunition boxes

Unprotected fuel tanks

Oil tanks

The layout of the Spitfire I. In common with almost all fighters in service in September 1939 it carried no armour or self-sealing tanks, though these would soon be fitted.

and at speeds near to its maximum in level flight. In a high speed dive its handling characteristics, particularly in the rolling plain, were known to be poor; as the aircraft neared 400 mph the ailerons became increasingly heavy, and above 430 mph they were almost immovable. But in 1939 the high speed dive was not considered relevant to the Spitfire's primary bomber-destroyer role, and no serious attempt was made to improve the aileron control. This fighter had a maximum level speed of just over 360 mph, an initial rate of climb of 2,530 feet per minute and it took just under 10 minutes to reach 20,000 feet (power for power a monoplane climbed less rapidly than a biplane, and it will be seen that this figure was little better than that of a 1934 fighter); the Spitfire was credited with a service ceiling of nearly 32,000 feet, though above 20,000 feet its performance deteriorated steadily.

In general the Spitfire I was comparable with, or superior to, those single-engined fighter designs in service with other air forces at the out-break of the war. Since the purpose of this section is to show the 'state of the art' of operational fighters in September 1939, rather than to describe every type of fighter in service with every air force, only those features of other fighters which were superior to their equivalent in the Spitfire will now be considered.

Running almost neck and neck with the Spitfire in the technological race was the German Messerschmitt 109 which had been in service since 1937 and in the summer of 1939 was being delivered in its E-1 version. This latest sub-type was powered by a Daimler Benz DB 601A, an inverted

V-12 of 33.9 litres capacity which developed 1,100 horse-power at just over 12,000 feet. The DB 601 featured two 'house specialities' of the Daimler Benz Company: direct fuel injection and a variable-speed supercharger drive. The advantages of injecting fuel directly into the cylinders, compared with the normal float carburettor system as fitted to the Merlin, were numerous: it provided better mixture control and distribution, since each cylinder received the same metered dose of fuel; since the injection took place when the inlet valves were closed, a backfire was impossible; and, most important of all for a fighter power plant, those with direct fuel injection were not sensitive to negative G conditions and in bunting manoeuvres they did not cut out (as did the Spitfire's Merlin). The penalties of direct fuel injection were the need for high standards of workmanship in the machining and assembly of the parts of the injection pumps, and meticulous cleanliness of the fuel; the German technicians and mechanics proved capable of achieving both of these. The other feature of the DB 601, the variable-speed hydraulic drive for the supercharger, was no less subtle; it provided the engine with greater boost at the higher altitudes where it was most needed, while a barometric capsule slowed the speed of the supercharger at low altitude and thus prevented overboosting and its attendant problems.

The airscrew fitted to the Messerschmitt 109E-1 was of the VDM variable pitch type, with which the blade angle could be set electrically from the cockpit; this infinitely variable system was better than the two-speed system fitted to the Spitfire, especially during the climb.

The armament of the Messerschmitt 109E-1 comprised two 20-mm cannon in the wings firing outside the propeller disc, and two 7.9-mm guns mounted on the engine and synchronised to fire through the airscrew. The Oerlikon MG FF cannon fired armour piercing, high explosive or incendiary shells each weighing about 4.5 ounces, at the rate of 350 per minute with a muzzle velocity of 1,900 feet per second. The Rheinmettall-Borsig MG 17 machine gun was generally comparable with the Browning fitted to the Spitfire, though in this installation there was a reduction in the rate of fire of about 10 per cent due to the action of the synchronisation gear which prevented fire while the propeller blades were in the way. The weight of fire of this aircraft was somewhat higher than that of the Spitfire though it was not, as we shall soon observe, the heaviest of those fighters in service in 1939.

The most modern fighter in service with the U.S. Army Air Corps and the French Armée de l'Air in September 1939 was the radial engined Curtiss P-36C (called the Hawk 75A in its export version). Although its general performance fell somewhat below those of the British and German fighters mentioned above the American fighter, with its finely harmonised controls and large mechanical advantage between stick and ailerons, was superior to either of them in its handling at high speeds. Also the P-36, in common with other American fighters of this period, carried a constant-speed propeller which adjusted the angle of the blades to the most efficient setting for the speed of the aircraft and the engine revolutions selected by the pilot; thus the engine and propeller operated at high efficiency over a wide range of conditions, and achieved automatically what the Messerschmitt pilots had to do manually and the Spitfire pilots could do only at the high

The best fighter in service with the U.S. Army Air Corps in the summer of 1939 was the Curtiss P-36C; designated the Hawk 75A, the export version of this fighter was in service with the French Armée de l'Air. The P-36C was powered by a 1,200 horse-power Pratt and Whitney Twin Wasp engine, and had a maximum speed of 311 mph at 10,000 feet. Armed with one .5-inch and three .3-inch machine guns, it had a loaded weight of 5,730 pounds.
U.S.A.A.F.

and low speeds ends of the performance envelope.

The most heavily armed fighter in service in September 1939 was the Russian Polikarpov I-16, a progressive development of an aircraft which had first entered service in 1934 and had fought in the Spanish Civil War. It had undergone a steady development programme but, having started out as the most advanced single-engined fighter in the world, it had gradually been overtaken in performance by the newer types. In terms of armament, however, it had never been surpassed. The I-16 Type 17, which appeared in 1938, carried two synchronised 7.62 ShKAS machine guns on top of the engine cowling and two 20-mm ShVAK cannon in the wings. The ShKAS had a rate of fire of 1,600 rounds per minute after synchronisation and a muzzle velocity of 2,700 feet per second; the ShVAK had a rate of fire of 800 rounds per minute and a muzzle velocity of 2,600 feet per second. In both cases these figures were better than those for any comparable weapon and they conferred upon the Type 17 a weight of fire of more than double that of the Messerschmitt 109E-1 and nearly three times that of the Spitfire I. The hefty punch of this tubby Russian fighter was years ahead of its time; not until 1941 would a western single-engined fighter enter service able to deliver a greater weight of fire. Moreover, unique amongst pre-war fighters, the I-16 carried armour protection round the pilot's

By a considerable margin the most powerfully armed single-engined fighter in the world in 1939 was the Russian Polikarpov I-16 Type 17, which carried two fast-firing 20-mm ShVAK cannon and two 7.62-mm ShKAS machine guns. However, the performance of this aircraft, the initial version of which had entered large-scale service in 1935, was less impressive and it had a maximum speed of well under 300 mph. The higher-powered Type 24 version, which entered service in 1940 and is depicted here, was powered by a 1,100 horse-power M 62 engine and had a maximum speed of 326 mph at sea level; carrying the same armament as the Type 17, the Type 24 had a loaded weight of 4,190 pounds. *I.W.M.*

Already obsolescent when it entered service in the Italian Air Force in the closing months of 1939, the Fiat CR 42 was to serve in the fighter role until well into 1942 and was the last of the biplane fighters to see large-scale operational use. Powered by an 840 horse-power Fiat A 74 engine, this aircraft had a maximum speed of 266 mph at 13,000 feet. Its armament comprised one 12.7-mm and one 7.7-mm machine guns, later two 12.7-mm machine guns, and it had a loaded weight of 5,040 pounds.
via F. Ghiselli

The best twin-engined fighter in service in September 1939 was the Messerschmitt 110C. Powered by two 1,100 horse-power Daimler-Benz DB 601s, this aircraft had a maximum speed of 336 mph at just under 20,000 feet. With a forward-firing armament of two 20-mm cannon and four 7.9-mm machine guns, and a single 7.9-mm gun for rear defence, it had a normal loaded weight of 13,290 pounds. *via Schliephake*

seat. Those who believe that the Russians were backward peasants prior to the Second World War, and advanced after it only because they were able to make use of German expertise, might care to ponder these points.

Of the twin-engined fighters in service at the beginning of the war the best, by a wide margin, was the German Messerschmitt 110C-1. Like the single-engined fighters already described it was a low-winged monoplane of all-metal construction; the two engines, Daimler Benz DB 601As similar to those fitted to the Messerschmitt 109E, were mounted in the conventional manner in nacelles on the wings which also housed the main undercarriage legs and wheels when they were retracted. The aircraft carried a wireless operator in addition to the pilot, necessary for long range air-to-ground communications at that time; during combat the wireless operator kept watch behind, and endeavoured to ward off attackers with his single rifle-calibre machine gun. The forward firing armament of the Messerschmitt 110C-1 comprised two 20-mm MG FF cannon and four 7.9-mm MG 17 machine guns, all grouped together neatly in the nose; this version carried no armour. The total fuel capacity, 280 Imp (335 U.S.) gallons, was housed in four unprotected tanks located in the wings between the fuselage and the engines; this was sufficient to provide the aircraft with an effective radius of action of about 340 miles. The Messerschmitt 110C-1 had a nor-

Opposite:
Although a more modern concept than the biplane CR 42, the Italian Fiat G 50 which entered service at about the same time showed no great advance in performance. Under-powered by the same engine as the CR 42, it had a maximum speed of 293 mph at 16,400 feet. With an armament of two 12.7-mm machine guns, it had a loaded weight of 5,560 pounds. *Fiat*

The layout of the Messerschmitt 110

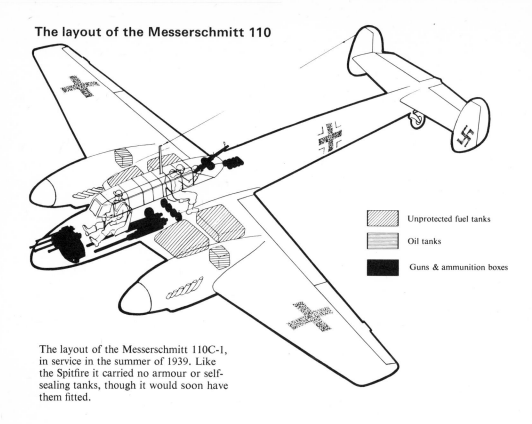

Unprotected fuel tanks

Oil tanks

Guns & ammunition boxes

The layout of the Messerschmitt 110C-1,
in service in the summer of 1939. Like
the Spitfire it carried no armour or self-
sealing tanks, though it would soon have
them fitted.

mal loaded weight of 13,290 pounds, which gave it a wing loading of 31 pounds per square foot and a power loading of 6 pounds per horse-power. It reached its maximum speed of 336 mph at just under 20,000 feet, had an initial rate of climb of 2,165 feet per minute and took just under 10.5 minutes to reach 20,000 feet. If the manoeuvrability of the Messerschmitt 110C-1 did not quite match up to that of the best single-engined fighters in 1939, its performance was far in advance of the other twin-engined fighters in service at that time: the French Potez 631, the Dutch Fokker G-1 and the British Bristol Blenheim.

The five fighters described above, the Spitfire, the Messerschmitt 109, the Curtiss P-36, the Polikarpov I-16 and the Messerschmitt 110 between them carried features representing the zenith of design, of the types in service at the beginning of the Second World War. We shall consider the path of evolution of the fighter aircraft during the years that followed, from the standpoints of layout, aerodynamics, structures, engines and armament.

The Shape of the Fighter

Throughout the Second World War one layout remained supreme for single-piston-engined fighters: the single-seat low-winged monoplane with a single fin and rudder, a fixed forward-firing armament and the engine mounted at the front of the fuselage driving a tractor airscrew. From the

beginning of the conflict this type established a clear superiority over those biplane fighters still in service, and as soon as possible the latter were replaced.

Both before and during the conflict, however, some designers did produce monoplane fighters outside the constraints of the layout described above. Only two of these were produced in quantity, the British Boulton Paul Defiant and the American P-39 Airacobra, and neither proved successful in the day fighter role.

The Defiant was a monoplane of conventional configuration, except that behind the pilot's cockpit there was a turret with a gunner and four rifle-calibre machine guns. As a bomber destroyer the turret fighter, as it was known at the time, seemed to offer advantages over the conventional fixed-gun fighter. In particular, it could formate to one side or in front of a bomber target and deliver sustained fire from directions where the latter's defensive fire and armour protection were least effective. It was a neat theory. But before the Defiant could establish the wisdom of it the Germans had learnt the folly of sending out bomber formations in daylight without fighter escort. And when it was confronted by conventional single-seat fighters, the relatively low performance and poor manoeuvrability of the Defiant made it an easy target. After a brief and blood-spattered career as a day fighter, the Defiant was relegated to night operations.

The other single-engined fighter design to deviate from the conventional layout which entered quantity production was the Bell P-39 Airacobra*;

Entering service in the early months of 1940, the Dewoitine 520 was the best fighter to serve in the French Armée de l'Air prior to the armistice. Powered by a 910 horse-power Hispano Suiza 12Y 45 engine, it had a maximum speed of 329 mph at 19,700 feet. With an armament of one 20-mm cannon and four 7.5-mm machine guns, the D.520 had a loaded weight of 6,130 pounds. *E. C. Armees*

* The successor to the Airacobra, the P-63 Kingcobra, also went into quantity production but its combat career was confined almost entirely to the ground attack role.

The only turret fighter to enter large-scale production, the Boulton Paul Defiant carried its entire armament of four .303-inch machine guns in the hydraulically powered turret above the centre fuselage. Built to a Royal Air Force specification for a bomber-destroyer, this type suffered severe losses when it came into contact with German single-seat fighters; after a disastrous initiation into combat, the type was relegated to night operations.

and at first glance even that *looked* conventional. In this aircraft the engine was buried in the fuselage *behind* the pilot's cockpit, and drove the propeller in the nose via a long shaft. This arrangement promised three advantages over the conventional one: firstly, because the engine was over the aircraft's centre of gravity, it appeared that manoeuvrability would be improved; secondly, because the weight of the engine was further aft, the cockpit could be moved further forward to allow the pilot a better view than was possible with a conventional fighter; and thirdly, the arrangement left the nose section clear for a concentrated gun battery comprising one 37-mm or 20-mm cannon and two machine guns as well as providing space in which to retract the nose wheel of the tricycle undercarriage (the Airacobra was the first single-engined fighter to go into service with this refinement, which provided greater ground stability and greatly improved handling). Alas, there were problems. The Airacobra was underpowered, which was no fault of the unconventional layout but it did much to aggravate the penalties of that layout. The rear fuselage had to be strengthened, and was therefore heavier than was normally the case, to prevent the engine breaking free during a crash landing and pulping the pilot as it moved forwards.

The unconventional Bell P-39 Airacobra, which had its engine mounted behind the cockpit. This arrangement left space in the nose for the nose wheel leg to retract, for two synchronised machine guns in the upper part of the nose and a 20-mm or 37-mm cannon firing through the propeller boss (the barrel of a 20-mm cannon can be seen protruding through the propeller shaft). The P-39D entered service in the U.S. Army Air Corps early in 1941; powered by a 1,150 horse-power Allison V-1710 engine, it had a maximum speed of 360 mph at 15,000 feet. Its armament comprised one 37-mm cannon, two .5-inch and four .3-inch machine guns and its normal loaded weight was 7,650 pounds. *U.S.A.A.F.*

The Yak-9 entered service in the Soviet Air Force at the end of 1942, and fought with that service until the end of the war. Powered by a 1,260 horse-power Klimov M-105 PF engine, it had a maximum speed of 368 mph at 16,400 feet. With an armament of one 20-mm cannon and two 12.7 mm machine guns the Yak-9 had a loaded weight of 6,330 pounds. *via Icare*

The Nakajima Ki 43 (Allied code-name 'Oscar') was the most used type of fighter in the Japanese Army during the initial stages of the war in the Pacific. The example depicted is the Ki 43-II, which entered service in the summer of 1943; unlike earlier Japanese fighters this version carried head and back armour for the pilot, and self-sealing fuel tanks. Powered by a 1,150 horse-power Ha 115 radial engine, the Ki 43-II had a maximum speed of 329 mph at 13,000 feet. Armed with two 12.7-mm machine guns, this fighter had a loaded weight of 5,300 pounds.

Added to this was the extra weight of the transmission shaft, 8 feet long and $2\frac{1}{2}$ inches in diameter, complete with a supporting bearing in the centre with its attendant mounting and lubrication system. With a wing loading of 36 pounds per square foot the P-39 was not a very manoeuvrable aircraft, and although its speed and climb performance at low and medium altitudes compared quite well with contemporary German and Japanese fighters it was never very popular as a fighter. Maintenance of the centrally-mounted engine presented a nightmare for the ground crews, who had to strip off several panels and often remove the rear canopy, the pilot's seat and back armour merely to perform routine engine servicing tasks. The engine operating controls and instrumentation lines presented a further problem, since from the front of the cockpit almost all of them had to go forward a little, down a little, back a lot and then up to reach the engine. After a relatively short career as a fighter, the Airacobra was relegated to the ground attack and training roles.

The shape of operational twin-engined fighters did not remain straight-jacketed to the same extent as with the single-engined types. Initially, however, the majority were of the same general layout as the Messerschmitt 110 though most carried only a single fin and rudder.

Then, in the summer of 1941, the Lockheed P-38 Lightning entered service in the U.S.A.A.F. This clean aircraft incorporated several unusual design features. The twin-boom layout was chosen so that the engines could be mounted in the front, and the main undercarriage legs and the exhaust-driven turbo-superchargers could go in the rear. (Turbo-superchargers are described in greater detail on page 67.) The Lightning featured a tricycle undercarriage, and the bubble-type canopy and short fuselage allowed the pilot an exceptional view above and behind. The Lightning had a wing loading which was, for its time, extremely high: 48.5 pounds

The Grumman F8F Bearcat, the most advanced carrier-borne fighter to be produced during the Second World War, entered service just too late to see action. Powered by a Pratt and Whitney R-2800-34W engine developing 2,100 horse-power, the F8F had a maximum speed of 421 mph at 19,700 feet. Armed with four .5-inch machine guns, the fighter had a normal loaded weight of 9,836 pounds. *Harold Martin*

During the Second World War the majority of twin-engined fighter types resulted from the modification of existing bomber types by the addition of a battery of forward-firing guns. Typical of these was the Junkers 88C, which carried three 20-mm cannon and three 7.9-mm machine guns in the nose. As a fighter this type enjoyed its greatest success at at night, though a few, like the C-6 version depicted belonging to *Kampfgeschwader 40*, were employed in daylight operations. The C-6 was powered by two 1,350 horse-power Jumo 211 J in-line liquid-cooled engines with annular radiators (see page 65), and had a maximum speed of 343 mph at 15,600 feet; the aircraft had a loaded weight of 26,000 pounds and carried a crew of three, and was the largest and heaviest day fighter to see service during the Second World War.

Entirely conventional in its layout was the twin-engined Bristol Beaufighter, the Royal Air Force's equivalent to the German Messerschmitt 110. The Mark VI version, illustrated, was powered by two 1,670 horse-power Bristol Hercules radials and had a maximum speed of 333 mph at 15,600 feet. It carried a forward firing armament of four 20-mm cannon and six .303-inch machine guns and a single .303-inch weapon for rear defence, and had a loaded weight of 21,600 pounds. *I.W.M.*

The most successful bomber-into-fighter conversion of all time was the de Havilland Mosquito; the Mark IV version, depicted here, entered service in the spring of 1943. This aircraft was powered by two 1,635 horse-power Rolls-Royce Merlin 25s and had a maximum speed of 380 mph at 13,000 feet. It carried a forward firing armament of four 20-mm cannon and four .303 inch machine guns, in addition to which it could carry bombs or rockets for ground attack work, and it had a normal loaded weight (without overload fuel) of 19,500 pounds. *C. Brown*

The Lockheed P-38J version of the Lightning, depicted here, entered service in the summer of 1942. The unusual twin-boom layout was chosen for this fighter because the booms provided a convenient housing for the turbo-superchargers and radiators, and their associated ducting. Powered by two 1,425 horse-power Allison V-1710's, the P-38J had a maximum speed of 414 mph at 25,000 feet. Armed with one 20-mm cannon and four .5-inch machine guns, it had a normal loaded weight of 17,500 pounds. *U.S.A.A.F.*

per square foot. To improve turning performance in combat later versions were modified so that their flaps could be lowered to an intermediate 8 degree down position; with the inside engine throttled back somewhat, the P-38 possessed low speed turning characteristics that were good by any standards (see page 110 .) The P-38F had a maximum speed of 395 mph and, with two 91 Imp (108 U.S.) gallon drop tanks it had an operational radius of 585 miles.

During the closing stages of the Second World War two twin-piston-engined fighter types went into production featuring unconventional layouts: the American P-82 Twin Mustang and the German Dornier 335. Both had performance figures which were close to the limits of what was possible using piston engines, but both were just too late to see action during the conflict.

The North American P-82 Twin Mustang comprised two Mustang fuselages joined together by a rectangular centre-wing and tailplane, and used standard Mustang components for the port and starboard outer wings. The 'twinning' of a conventional single-engined fighter in this way was a simple low-risk method of producing a twin-engined fighter in a hurry using proven components; design work on the Twin Mustang began in January 1944 and the first prototype was flying before the end of April 1945. Other designers gave serious thought to 'twinning' as a means of increasing the range of fighters, but the Twin Mustang was the only one

Just about to enter service at the end of the war, the beautifully clean de Havilland Hornet incorporated many of the lessons the company had learnt from the earlier Mosquito. The Hornet I was powered by two 2,030 horse-power Rolls-Royce Merlin 130 series engines, and attained a maximum speed of 472 mph at 22,000 feet. It carried an armament of four 20-mm cannon and had a loaded weight of 17,700 pounds. *C. Brown*

Too late to see action during the Second World War, the Grumman F7F Tigercat was the first twin-engined fighter to enter service able to operate from aircraft carriers. Powered by two 2,100 horse-power Pratt and Whitney R-2800-34W engines, the F7F had a maximum speed of 435 mph at 22,200 feet. It carried an armament of four 20-mm cannon and four .5-inch machine guns, and had a normal loaded weight of 21,720 pounds. *U.S. Navy*

to go into production. Its two fuselages acted as end-plates to increase the efficiency of the joining wing, and the carriage of two pilots abreast of each other 14 feet apart provided excellent all-round vision with each man able to cover most of his partner's blind areas. The P-82 had a maximum speed of 482 mph at 25,000 feet.

In the same performance category as the Twin Mustang was the Dornier 335, an equally unconventional aircraft featuring a tandem layout for its engines with one in front and one behind the cockpit; the front one drove a conventional tractor propeller, while the rear one drove a pusher propeller at the rear of the aircraft. To prevent the rear propeller from striking the ground during take off or landing the Do 335 had a cruciform fin

The unconventional North American P-82 Twin Mustang comprised two Mustang fuselages joined together by a rectangular centre wing and tailplane; the outer wings were standard Mustang components; like the Hornet, the P-82 was just too late for the Second World War. Powered by two 1,860 horse-power Packard V-1650 engines (licence-built Merlins) the P-82 had a maximum speed of 482 mph at 25,100 feet. Armed with six .5-inch machine guns, it had a normal loaded weight of 19,100 pounds. *North American*

arrangement, with a sprung bumper at the base of the lower fin. The positioning of the second propeller at the rear of the aircraft conferred several aerodynamic advantages over the conventional tractor layout. Firstly, since there was no part of the aircraft structure behind it, none of the rear propeller's thrust was dissipated in skin friction; for this reason, although it was fitted with two engines of equal power, the Do 335 was faster on the rear engine with the front propeller feathered than it was on the front engine with the rear propeller feathered. Secondly, there was the advantage of being able to fit two engines into an aircraft for the drag penalty of only one. Thirdly, unique amongst production twin-engined fighters of the Second World War period, the Do 335 could fly with one engine stopped with no resultant assymetric handling problem; since many hundreds of aircraft were lost during that conflict in crashes following attempted assymetric landings, this was no small advantage. To save the pilot from an almost certain head-ectomy if he tried to abandon the aircraft through the disc of the rear propeller, the Do 335 carried a primitive ejector seat backed up by a system of explosive bolts to blow away the propeller. The Do 335A had a maximum speed of 474 mph at just over 21,000 feet.

By the middle of 1942 both the liquid fuelled rocket and the turbo-jet engine had reached the point where they could be considered as power plants for operational fighters. And with this change, the layout constraints imposed by the piston engine disappeared. The result of this sudden free-

dom was that of the seven types of jet fighter to enter large-scale production in Germany, Great Britain and the U.S.A. before the end of the war, six featured layouts unique to themselves.

The first of the jet fighters to enter operational service was the German rocket-propelled Messerschmitt 163, which began flying combat missions in May 1944. Alone amongst wartime operational fighters, it featured no tail plane. Nor was there an undercarriage in the conventional sense; the Me 163 took off on a small dolly, which was jettisoned once it was airborne, and landed on a simple skid. A feature of the rocket motor was its voracious appetite for fuel and the tank capacity of 333 Imp (398 U.S.) gallons was sufficient for only *four minutes* running at full power; the fuel load made up more than half the 'Me 163's take-off weight of just over 8,700 pounds, and for safety reasons the tanks had to be emptied before landing. The result was an exceptionally high variation in wing loading during the flight: for take off this was just under 43 pounds per square foot and for landing it was under 22 pounds per square foot. The Me 163B had a maxi-

Featuring two 1,900 horse-power Daimler-Benz DB 603E engines in a unique tandem layout, the Dornier 335A had a maximum speed of 474 mph at 21,300 feet. It carried a basic armament of one-30 mm and two 15-mm cannon, and had a normal loaded weight of 21,160 pounds. As in the case of the British and American high performance twin-piston-engined types, the Do 335 was just too late to see action.

Powered by a 3,750 pound thrust Walter 509C rocket motor, the Messerschmitt 163B was the first jet propelled aircraft to go into action. Moreover this tail-less aircraft was the fastest fighter type to go into service during the Second World War, with a sustained maximum operational speed of just under 560 mph. It carried a built-in armament of two 20-mm or two 30-mm cannon, and had a loaded weight of 8,707 pounds. *via Ethell*

mum operational speed of just under 560 mph and an initial rate of climb of 16,000 feet per minute, which sounds marvellous. But, as we shall see later (on page 74) the constraints imposed by the rocket motor were such that the fighter was able to achieve little.

The second jet fighter to become operational was the German Messerschmitt 262. Powered by two turbo-jets this was a much more conservative design than the Me 163 and it featured a layout similar to that of a conventional twin-piston-engined fighter, with the engines in nacelles under the wings. The British Gloster Meteor, with a layout which was almost exactly similar, became operational shortly afterwards.

Of the single turbo-jet designs, the first to enter large-scale production was the German Heinkel 162. This aircraft had its engine mounted on top of the fuselage, allowing short and efficient inlet and exhaust ducting, and twin fins at the rear out of the jet efflux. Alone amongst production wartime fighters the He 162 featured a high wing which, situated well behind the cockpit, allowed the pilot a view which would have been excellent but for the engine immediately behind his canopy which effectively blocked vision in the vitally important sector to the rear and above. A further disadvantage of the position of the engine above the fuselage was that during the landing approach, with the nose well up, any disturbed airflow

Interior of the cockpit of the Me 163, showing the simplicity of the engine controls and instrumentation when propulsion was by rocket. *Crown Copyright*

The first turbo-jet engined aircraft to go into action was the Messerschmitt 262. Powered by two 1,980 pound thrust Jumo 004B engines, it had a maximum speed of 540 mph at 20,000 feet. It carried a built-in armament of four 30-mm cannon which could be supplemented by air-to-air rockets (the aircraft in the photograph has launchers for two Wgr 21 rockets under the nose); the normal loaded weight (without rockets) was 14,100 pounds. *via Girbig*

over the cockpit was liable to cause compressor stalling and a possible flame-out; if this happened there was little time for recovery before the aircraft hit the ground.

The American Lockheed P-80 Shooting Star was a low-wing design with its single turbo-jet buried in the fuselage behind the cockpit, drawing its air from intakes mounted on each side of the fuselage and exhausting via a jet pipe which ended just under the tail. The relatively long intake ducting resulting from this layout required careful design, and early examples of the P-80 suffered from duct rumble and other feeding problems especially during flight at low airspeeds. Following extensive wind tunnel tests a boundary layer bleed system was designed for the intakes, and this cured

The Gloster Meteor I, which entered service in the summer of 1944 shortly after the Me 262, was the first jet propelled aircraft to enter service in the Royal Air Force. Powered by two 1,700 pound thrust Rolls-Royce Welland engines the Meteor I had a maximum speed of 410 mph at 30,000 feet and weighed 11,800 pounds loaded. Just before the end of the war the Meteor III entered service (depicted); powered by two 2,000 pound thrust Rolls-Royce Derwent I engines it had a maximum speed of 493 mph at 30,000 feet and weighed 13,300 pounds. All versions of the Meteor carried an armament of four 20-mm cannon. *C. Brown*

most of the problems. The P-80A had a maximum speed of 558 mph at sea level, and an initial rate of climb of 4,580 feet per minute.

To get the advantages of a buried engine in the fuselage, without the penalties of long intake and exhaust ducting, the British de Havilland company chose the twin-boom layout for its Vampire fighter. As in the case of the P-38 Lightning this layout resulted in superb all-round visibility for the pilot. The Vampire I had a wing loading of only 32 pounds per square foot, which made it one of the most lightly-loaded of the fighters of the late war period and also one of the most manoeuvrable. The Vampire I had a maximum speed of 531 mph at 17,500 feet and an initial rate of climb of 4,200 feet per minute.

The first single turbo-jet fighter to go into large scale production was the Heinkel 162, an emergency type which was designed, built and flown within the remarkably short period of only ninety days. Some aspects of the type's handling characteristics were poor, however, and although nearly 200 had been delivered to the Luftwaffe before the war ended it was not considered ready for operations. Powered by a 1,764 pound thrust BMW 003E the He 162A-2 had a maximum sustained speed of 521 mph at 19,700 feet; for short bursts of up to 30 seconds the engine could deliver 2,028 pounds of thrust, allowing a maximum speed of 562 mph at 19,700 feet to be attained and held for about 15 seconds. Armed with two 20-mm cannon, the fighter weighed 6,184 pounds loaded. *via Schliephake*

The Lockheed P-80A Shooting Star was on the point of entering large-scale service in the US Army Air Force when the war ended. Powered by a 3,850 pound thrust General Electric J 33, it had a maximum speed of 558 mph at sea level; armed with six .5-inch guns, it weighed 11,700 pounds loaded without external fuel.

Also about to enter service when the war ended was the de Havilland Vampire I. On the 3,100 pound thrust of a de Havilland Goblin II engine, this aircraft had a maximum speed of 531 mph at 17,500 feet; it carried an armament of four 20-mm cannon, and had a loaded weight of 8,578 pounds. *C. Brown*

The only fighter type to go into service powered by both a piston engine and a turbo-jet was the Ryan FR-1 Fireball; the first U.S. Navy squadron to receive this aircraft, VF 66, was working up for carrier operations with it when the war ended. Powered by a 1,425 horse-power Wright R-1820 and a 1,600 pound thrust General Electric J 31, the Fireball had a maximum speed of 426 mph at 18,100 feet. It carried an armament of four .5-inch machine guns, and had a loaded weight of 9,862 pounds. The Fireball is depicted showing off its party piece: flying on its turbo-jet, with the piston engine stopped. *Ryan*

The American Ryan Fireball, the seventh of the jet fighters in production at the end of the war, was unique in that it employed both a piston engine and a turbo-jet. Due to poor throttle response the early jet engines by themselves were unsuitable for carrier-based aircraft, since the pilot could not climb away quickly enough if he had to abandon a landing approach at the last moment. To overcome this problem, while still getting the high performance of the turbo-jet engine, the Ryan Company designed its Fireball fighter around a 1,425 horse-power Wright Cyclone radial engine in the nose, and a 1,600 pound thrust General Electric J-31 turbo-jet in the centre fuselage exhausting under the tail. The combination proved to be an effective one, and the Fireball had a maximum speed of 426 mph at 18,000 feet and an initial rate of climb of 4,800 feet per minute.

Of the seven jet fighter types described above only three, the Me 163, the Me 262 and the Meteor, saw action. When the war ended operational units were preparing to go into action with the Heinkel 162 and the Ryan Fireball, while the first production batches of the de Havilland Vampire and Lockheed P-80 had been delivered.

Improving the Performance

By September 1940, a year after the outbreak of war, the true situation regarding air-to-air combat had become clear: the 'state of the art' fighter, with the aid of ground control using radar, was more than a match for the 'state of the art' bomber. The fighter designs of 1934 had achieved what their builders had wanted of them. Yet there was no time for anyone to rest on his laurels. Now bombers rarely operated over enemy territory by day unless they had fighter escort. This, in turn, meant that fighter-versus-fighter combat, which had seemed both unnecessary and unlikely before the war, now became the fighter's primary role. The dogfight, which many had thought as outdated as trench warfare, was suddenly as important as it had ever been.

If fighters were to fight each other as well as bombers, then additional qualities would be required of them. A high maximum speed and a high rate of climb were both still of the utmost importance; but to these were now added the requirement for good handling characteristics at high altitude and in the dive, and a high rate of roll (this was more important than a small turning circle, because it enabled a fighter to change direction rapidly to take aim or shake off pursuit). Also a large radius of action, to enable fighters to escort bombers deep into enemy territory, assumed a new importance.

The Spitfire remained in production from before the beginning of the war to well after the end. During the conflict it was developed to an exceptional degree, and in 1945 it was still a potent fighting machine; an examination of the aerodynamic changes made to it will, therefore, serve to exemplify the general pattern of fighter development during the period. The initial improvements were all fairly simple ones: a slight increase in engine power, the fitting of constant speed propellers and the fitting of metal instead of fabric covered ailerons to improve handling at high speeds. From then on the evolution of the Spitfire can be summed up broadly as follows. A series of engines of progressively greater power were fitted, and these required progressively larger propellers to convert this power into thrust; the prototype Spitfire had had a two-bladed propeller, by 1939 there were three blades, by 1942 four blades and by 1944 Spitfires were flying with five-bladed propellers. Aerodynamically, the propeller produced an effect on stability similar to that one would expect from a large cruciform fin on the nose, while the rotating slipstream round the fuselage tried to screw the aircraft into a roll; with the fitting of larger engines and propellers these effects became more serious and had to be corrected by increases in the size of the fin and tailplane, to provide the necessary straightening moment.

Simultaneously, airframes became much cleaner. The effect on maximum speed of various small changes to the airframe may be seen from the following results, obtained during a trial in 1943 with a Spitfire V: maximum speed of standard aircraft, 357 mph; with multi-ejector exhausts fitted in place of the older 'fish tail' type, plus 7 mph; with the carburettor intake ice-guard removed, plus 8 mph; with a whip radio aerial in place of the older mast-type, plus $\frac{1}{2}$ mph; with a new type of rear-view mirror with a front fairing, plus 3 mph; with the ammunition cartridge case and link ejector chutes cut flush instead of protruding beneath the wing, plus 1 mph; with the leading edge of the wing smoothed out by stopping, rubbing down, painting and polishing, plus 6 mph; with additional polishing of the rest of the aircraft using wax, plus 3 mph. Together, these individually small changes increased the speed of the Spitfire V from 357 mph to $385\frac{1}{2}$ mph, a difference of $28\frac{1}{2}$ mph. The retractable tail wheel, fitted to later marks of the Spitfire, was worth about 4 mph at 400 mph.

If we compare the Mark 21 Spitfire, the model in production at the close of the war, with the Mark I in production at the beginning, we can get a fair picture of the effects of the development of this fighter during the conflict. In each case the figures given are those of the Mark 21, and their relation to those of the Mark I are given in brackets: engine power 2,035 h.p. (nearly double); normal loaded weight 9,900 pounds (nearly three-quarters more), at which the wing loading was 40.5 pounds per square foot (two-

thirds greater) and the power loading was 4.9 pounds per horse-power (4 per cent better); initial rate of climb was 4,900 feet per minute (nearly double), maximum speed was 450 mph (greater by one-quarter) and the service ceiling was 43,000 feet (greater by one-third). The maximum take-off weight of the Spitfire 21, carrying a full 170 Imp (202 U.S.) gallon drop tank, was 11,290 pounds; this was greater than that of the Spitfire I by a weight the equivalent of thirty 12-stone passengers each with 40 pounds of luggage!

One important airframe change which was not incorporated in the Spitfire during the Second World War was the so-called 'laminar flow' wing. This was a wing with an exceptionally fine finish: the surface roughness had to be less than .0005 of an inch and the maximum wave allowance

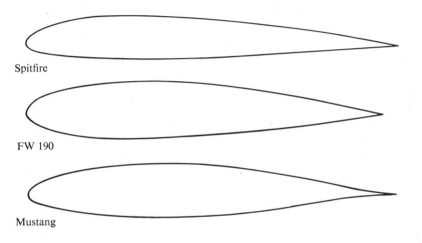

Spitfire

FW 190

Mustang

Wing sections. Top, the Spitfire: the thinnest section to be used for a Second World War fighter, this section had an exceptionally high threshold of compressibility. Centre, the Focke Wulf 190: a typical section for a fighter of the mid-war period. Bottom, the P-51 Mustang: although this high-speed laminar flow section gave a lower drag than the other two when it was in good condition and highly polished, its efficiency fell rapidly if particles of dirt or crushed insects adhered to the leading edge; moreover, this section had a somewhat lower threshold of compressibility than the thin section of the Spitfire.

was .0001 of an inch in any two inches of surface. This fineness of finish was combined with a high speed aerofoil section, with its thickest point about half way back from the leading edge (rather than a third of the way back, in a conventional aerofoil). The first aircraft operational with the laminar flow wing was the North American P-51 Mustang, which entered service in the RAF in the summer of 1942. Later, re-engined with a Rolls-Royce Merlin with a two-stage supercharger, the Mustang became one of the outstanding fighters of the war. The effect of the laminar flow wing can be seen if the performance of the P-51B Mustang is compared with that of the Spitfire IX; the comparison is valid, because the two aircraft were powered by almost exactly the same type of Merlin. In terms of wing span and area the Mustang's wing was closely comparable with that of the Spitfire; the latter's wing was 2 inches longer and about 4 per cent greater in area. Yet in spite of the similarity in wing dimensions and engine power, and the considerably greater weight of the Mustang (about a quarter greater), the latter was approximately 20 mph faster than the Spitfire IX for any given cruising power setting of the engine, and about 30 mph faster at maximum speed. The main factors responsible for this were the laminar flow wing and the high speed aerofoil.

As has been mentioned earlier in this section, one of the factors that was required by fighter pilots was the highest possible diving speed while maintaining full control. By 1943 the latest fighters were able to reach speeds during dives which were beyond the threshold of compressibility; the sound barrier was beginning to rear its ugly head. The effects of compressibility varied from aircraft to aircraft; on fighters with thick wings the threshold came quite early, at about .7 Mach (about 500 mph at 20,000 feet, depending upon temperature). As the aircraft advanced further over the threshold the effects became more and more serious as the shock waves upset the airflow over the wings and affected fore and aft stability and gradually the pilot lost control over his aircraft. This placed the pilot in a difficult situation, since during these steep dives at angles of 60 or 70 degrees he was losing height at a rate of about 40,000 feet per minute; it was not difficult to lose as much as 10,000 feet during the uncontrollable part of the dive, and to this had to be added a further 10,000 feet for a safe recovery. Those who went too far beyond their aircraft's compressibility threshold found that they regained control at an altitude too low to pull out of their dive. Nobody did that twice.

Two American fighters, the P-38 Lightning and the P-47 Thunderbolt, suffered severe compressibility effects at speeds below .7 Mach. In the case of the latter the problem was aggravated by the fact that a sudden reduction in engine power during the dive caused a *nose-down* trim change, which steepened the dive and increased the speed still further. To assist the recovery from uncontrollable dives, later versions of both aircraft were fitted with small dive-recovery flaps under their wings about a third of the way back from the leading edge; when lowered they caused a nose-up pitching moment, which pulled the fighter out of the dive. The dive-recovery flaps on the Thunderbolt were quite small, each with an area of 1.7 square feet, and their maximum extension angle was only 20 degrees.

In the mid-war generation of fighters the phenomenon of compressibility was one which could, with a little care, usually be avoided in combat. With the first generation of jet fighters, however, there was no such simple way round the problem. At full throttle in a shallow dive at an angle of 20 degrees from 26,000 feet, the Messerschmitt 262 was well beyond its compressibility threshold before it had descended through 7,000 feet. The threshold was reached at .83 Mach at which point the nose started to drop and a backward pull on the stick of about 30 pounds was required to hold the aircraft straight. As the speed increased still further a violent buffeting set in and the aircraft became progressively more nose-heavy, until at .86 Mach (a true airspeed of about 620 mph at 19,000 feet) a backwards force of about 100 pounds on the stick was required to prevent the Messerschmitt bunting over into an uncontrollable vertical dive.

One aid which would have been useful to jet fighter pilots at this time was the Machmeter, which gave an immediate reading of the relationship of the aircraft's speed with that of sound for the altitude at which it was flying; but this device did not come into general use until after the war. In the case of the Me 262 the Luftwaffe High Command imposed an airspeed limitation of 595 mph (True), and gave strict orders that pilots were not to exceed it; the similar airspeed limitation for the Me 163 was 559 mph.

Somewhat worse off than the two German jet fighters from the point of

EE211/G

view of compressibility threshold were the Mark I and Mark III versions of the British Meteor. These suffered airflow breakaway at the outboard nacelle-wing junctions at Mach .74, resulting in severe wing buffeting. Following extensive wind tunnel tests a set of lengthened engine nacelles was produced and flown on a Meteor just before the end of the war; these improved matters considerably and delayed the onset of compressibility, and the aircraft was taken to a new limit of .84 Mach. After the war production Meteors with the longer nacelles were operated to a service limitation of .8 Mach.

Provided there was no aerodynamic weakness in the design which brought on the effects of compressibility at a lower figure, it was the shape and thickness of the wing which usually decided the limiting Mach number. Before the end of the war the Germans had discovered that the compressibility threshold could be delayed considerably by the use of sharply swept-back wings; and several of their projected fighters at the end of the war featured such wings. However, to get any major improvement in this way it is necessary to sweep back the wing by 35 to 40 degrees. So it can be seen that the 18 degree leading edge sweep back on the Me 262, or the 27 degrees on the Me 163 was not sufficient to delay the onset of compressibility by any great amount; the two German fighters were good in this respect because they were clean aircraft, not because their wings were bent back a little.

As has been mentioned, the effects of compressibility could be delayed either by sweeping back the wing or by using a very thin wing. It was the latter which gave the Spitfire a Mach performance unequalled during the Second World War and for some time after it. The Spitfire had the thinnest

A Meteor I carrying the lengthened engine nacelles (compare the size with those of the aircraft on page 36); this was the first time ever that a service aircraft was modified to raise its limiting Mach number, and in the case of the Meteor I it raised the limit from .74 to .84 Mach.

Before the end of the war the Germans had discovered that the onset of compressibility could be delayed by the fitting of sharply swept-back wings.

However, the 18 degree sweep-back of the wings of the Me 262 was insufficient to give much improvement in this respect.

wing of any of the fighters of this period, with a root thickness of only 13 per cent of the chord (this compared with 14.7 per cent for the Me 163 and 16 per cent for the Mustang). Once its original fabric covered ailerons had been replaced by metal ones, and the aircraft had been cleaned up a little with a retractable tail wheel, the Spitfire had an outstanding Mach performance. During a trial at Farnborough in 1943 a slightly modified Spitfire XI (a reconnaissance version of the Mark IX fighter) was taken to .9 Mach, a truly magnificent achievement for the time.

Had the war gone on and combats between jet fighters become commonplace, it is likely that the problem of compressibility would have had a considerable effect on fighter tactics. In the past, the rule had been to try to get above one's opponent and dive on him with the advantage of speed. Now, with fighters almost able to reach their maximum controllable speed in level flight, excess height could become an embarrassment because even a shallow dive could place the aircraft beyond its compressibility threshold. To overcome this problem British and American designers fitted their jet fighters with dive brakes to enable their pilots to hold down the speed during the descent; Willi Messerschmitt, who was more interested in producing a vehicle for destroying the enemy bombers than one for jousting with his fighters, did not bother.

Dive brakes fitted to the Meteor, to enable it to carry out a high speed descent without exceeding its compressibility limits.

The Mitsubishi A6M2 Zero, nearest the camera, was the mainstay of the Japanese Navy's fighter arm during the initial stages of the war in the Pacific. Unarmoured and lightly constructed, it was able to absorb little battle damage. On the other hand its range performance was quite remarkable for a single-engined fighter of the early war period; with a 73 Imp (86 U.S.) gallon drop tank, it was capable of operating at distances of over 500 miles from its base. Powered by a 950 horse-power Nakajima Sakae 12 engine, this fighter had a maximum speed of 331 mph at 14,900 feet. Armed with two 20-mm cannon and two 7.7-mm machine guns, it had a loaded weight of 5,313 pounds. *U.S.N.*

Extending the Reach

At the beginning of the Second World War the single-engined fighters in service were, without exception, short-ranging machines able to operate at a high speed cruise within a radius of action of only about 160 miles. By the beginning of 1941, however, simple drop tanks were in use or planned for almost all operational fighter types.

Using fuel from their drop tanks for the initial part of the flight, and by careful fuel handling and cruising at low speeds, fighter pilots were able to operate at quite remarkable distances from their bases. For example the lightweight Japanese A6M2 Zero, powered by a small engine developing a maximum of only 950 horse-power, was able to carry the not exceptional total of 114 Imp (137 U.S.) gallons of fuel internally and 73 Imp (86 U.S.) gallons in a drop tank. By cruising at speeds around 135 mph on lean mixture at low engine revolutions, however, it was possible to reduce consumption of a 'clean' Zero to about 18 Imp (22 U.S.) gallons of fuel per hour. Such flying methods, employed during the early stages of the Pacific war by pilots well practised in their use, enabled Zeroes based on Formosa to escort bombers as far afield as Manila in the Philippines – which represented a radius of action of about 500 miles.

Of course, the distance from their base to which fighters are operated depends to a large extent on the risks a commander is prepared to take. The slow-cruising Zeroes in the example quoted above would certainly have had a thin time had they been 'bounced' by enemy fighters while en route. However, the Japanese were more ready than most to take risks with men and equipment in order to secure a military gain, and they did not shrink from planning flights which cut deeply into an aircraft's fuel reserves.

To see how rapidly the various safety factors and allowances could whittle away the combat radius of a fighter, let us examine the U.S. Navy figures for the F4U-1 Corsair carrier fighter. With a full internal fuel load

Although several nations considered float-plane fighters, the Japanese Nakajima A6M2-N (Allied code-name 'Rufe') was the only such aircraft to go into service in quantity during the Second World War. Developed from the A6M2 Zero and powered by the same type of engine and carrying a similar armament, the performance of the A6M2-N suffered as a result of the weight and drag of the floats; its maximum speed was only 270 mph at 16,400 feet. The type's service career was not marked by great success: it proved greatly inferior to Allied land-based fighters, and lacked the necessary performance to catch the more modern Allied bombers. *U.S.N.*

of 300 Imp (361 U.S.) gallons, plus a 145 Imp (175 U.S.) gallon drop tank, this aircraft was credited with a maximum range of 2,215 miles cruising at 178 mph. Terms such as 'maximum range' need to be defined, however, and this was the official U.S. Navy definition:

Maximum range: this is a design yardstick and for this reason it does *not* include warm-up, take-off or reserve fuel. However it does take account of the horizontal distance travelled and the fuel used during the climb to and the descent from the designated altitude. Ammunition and drop tanks are carried the full distance in calculating the maximum range.

From the above it can be seen that the term 'maximum range' was virtually meaningless in any operational context. Halving this figure and subtracting a little for bad luck would leave one with a very shaky combat radius. In fact, the practical combat radius of the Corsair with this same fuel load was only 425 miles – about one-*fifth* of the theoretical maximum range. So again it is necessary to define the terms used, and in the U.S. Navy 'practical combat radius' was defined as follows:

Practical combat radius is based on 20 min. warm-up and idling; 1 min. take-off; 10 min. rendezvous at 60% normal sea-level power (NSP) and auto-rich (mixture); climb to 15,000 feet at 60% NSP; cruise-out at 15,000 feet at speed for maximum range and auto-lean; drop external tanks; 20 minutes combat at 15,000 feet at full military power; descent, cruise back at sea level at speed for maximum range and auto-lean; 60 minutes rendezvous, landing and reserve at speed for maximum range on auto-lean. Radius includes distance covered in climb, but not in descent.

The allowance of 20 minutes for warm-up and idling might seem excessive but in terms of carrier operations, when a whole task force might have to turn into wind to allow the aircraft to take off, this was not so. Similarly the 60 minutes reserve to get back, find the carrier and land on was necessary to allow for the vagaries of the wind and the weather; without this fuel in hand a rain squall over the carrier, or a crash blocking the deck, might otherwise result in all or part of an air group having to ditch.

In the case of the F4U-1 Corsair, the combat radius was further limited by the amount of *protected* fuel that was available when it went into combat. Only the main fuselage tank was self-sealing; the wing tanks and drop tank were not. The plan was, therefore, for the Corsair to cruise out to its combat area using first the fuel in the wing tanks, then the fuel out of the drop tank. When it reached its practical combat radius from its carrier the Corsair still had 112 Imp (134 U.S.) gallons remaining in its drop tank, which had to be released if the aircraft was to go into combat immediately; or the fuel could be used for a 2½-hour patrol at the limit of the practical combat radius. So much for the practical radius of action figures for the Corsair; they illustrate well the sort of operational constraints imposed by the need to operate aircraft in wartime without undue hazard. If a commander wished to conduct operations at distances beyond the practical combat radius of his aircraft he could do so, but first he had to ascertain that the weather and other conditions were favourable and the fuel reserves would not be really needed.

When it came to operations at great distances from base no single-

A F4U Corsair carrier fighter demonstrating its hydraulically powered wing folding system. In addition to wing folding, naval fighters carried catapult spools and an arrester hook, with local strengthening of the airframe to enable it to withstand the increased loads; also, the undercarriage needed to be stronger than that of an equivalent land-based aircraft, to withstand the greater shock of deck landings. By the end of the war the necessary deck landing equipment and strengthening amounted to about 4 per cent of the loaded weight of a carrier fighter (some 480 pounds for the 12,039 pound Corsair). Moreover the profile drag due to the catapult spools and the arrester hook, combined with the leak drag along the break of the folding wings, added about 10 per cent to the drag of naval fighters. In general terms these penalties resulted in a naval fighter being about 5 per cent slower (20 mph at 400 mph) and having a rate of climb 12 per cent lower, than a non-naval fighter of similar shape and power. *C. Brown*

engined fighter, and few twin-engined fighters, came close to the capability
of the later versions of the P-51 Mustang. This exceptionally clean fighter
(see page 43) had a voluminous capacity of 234 Imp (267 U.S.) gallons of
internal fuel. With two 90 Imp (108 U.S.) gallon drop tanks it was able
to furnish escort over the target for bombers attacking Posen (now Poznan
in Poland), more than 700 miles from the bases in Britain. With the Mustang able to undertake maximum radius sorties lasting over seven hours,
the limit to effectiveness became human rather than mechanical: how long
could a fighter pilot maintain the necessary concentration, sealed in his
cramped cockpit? It was to overcome this problem that the North American company produced its Twin Mustang (see page 32); with two pilots
to share the work load, operational effectiveness during very long flights
was greatly increased. After the war a stripped Twin Mustang fitted with
four large external tanks demonstrated how far the limits had been pushed
when it covered the 4,978 miles from Honolulu to New York in 14 hours
31 minutes at an average speed of 343 mph. It was a record for unrefuelled
distance flying by a fighter-type aircraft which will probably never be
broken.

The Structure of the Fighter

The structures of most high performance fighters at the beginning of the
war were of all-metal stressed skin construction, with fabric covering for
the control surfaces. In each case the metal used was aluminium, or an
alloy of aluminium. Pure aluminium was used in sheet form for fairings,
cowlings and other lightly loaded sections, where its suitability for welding
simplified fabrication. Where greater strength was required aluminium
alloyed with a small amount of copper, Duralamin, was used. Where
strength combined with good resistance to corrosion was required,
Alclad was used; this was Duralamin sheeting with a very thin outside
coating of pure aluminium. To take the case of a typical early wartime
fighter, the Messerschmitt 109E, the thickness of the wing skinning varied
from 1.4 mm near the root to .7 mm at the tip and the fuselage was covered
mainly in sheeting .6 mm thick. During the course of the conflict the skin
became progressively thicker as greater structural strength was demanded,
and the Me 262 at the end of the conflict carried wing skinning 2 mm thick.

An example of all-metal stressed skin construction: the rear fuselage of the Messerschmitt 109E.

Since the skin took much of the stress, the use of stressed skin construction conferred considerable advantages in strength and stiffness. This form of construction remained the most popular and successful for fighters during the Second World War and, indeed, since.

During the war all of the combatant nations faced actual or potential shortages of aluminium, and in several countries designers drew up plans for fighters made of wood. The most successful wooden aircraft were the British de Havilland Mosquito, a twin-engined aircraft originally designed as a high speed unarmed bomber but which also made a remarkably fine long-range fighter, and the Russian Lavochkin series of fighters. In each case ingenious arrangements of cross ply had to be used to overcome the adverse effects of grain. De Havilland developed a form of sandwich construction comprising two thin layers of plywood round a thick core of balsa wood; Lavochkin employed a similar form of sandwich, using bakelite as the core. Wood was more vulnerable than metal to the effects of

Constructed mainly of wood, the Russian Lavochkin La-5 FN entered large-scale service in the summer of 1943. Powered by a 1,640 horse-power Shvetsov M-82FN engine, it had a maximum speed of 402 mph at sea level It carried an armament of two 20-mm cannon and loaded weighed 7,406 pounds. *via Icare*

the weather, and as a result wooden aircraft tended to last a shorter time. It could be argued, however, that in wartime this did not matter very much; then, whatever their construction, combat aircraft had short lives (this was particularly so under the rigorous conditions of the Russian front, where Soviet fighters had an average combat life of only about *eighty* flying hours).

During the Second World War all of the combatant nations came to accept the need for armour protection for the pilot and other vital parts of their fighter aircraft. Prior to the conflict, this had been the subject of some discussion. The general consensus of informed opinion was that, since sufficient armour could not be carried to make protection complete, it was wiser to strengthen the attack as much as possible with guns and ammunition rather than waste payload and performance on what was, at best, an imperfect passive defence. The figures speak for themselves: to provide protection against 20 mm armour-piercing rounds fired from short range, steel plating 45 mm thick was required; merely to have provided back and head protection for the pilot with such plating would have meant incurring a weight penalty of about 350 pounds. Clearly full protection against this 'worst case' situation was out of the question for lightly built high-performance fighters. The war soon showed the value of even partial protection of the pilot and vulnerable parts of the aircraft, however.

Since complete protection was not possible within the weight constraints of fighter design, the designers had to do the best they could with what was available. In most fighters there was in front of the pilot an engine which, even if it suffered damage in the process, did provide the pilot with an excellent shield against fire from ahead. The lightest form of protection was the use of Duralamin plates of about 4 mm thickness in selected parts of the structure, to act as deflector plates; these were often sufficient to cause the ricochet of light or heavy machine gun rounds striking at a shallow angle or from long range. Another form of protection was the use of toughened glass panels of approximately 50 mm thickness for the pilot's windscreen (this was referred to by its makers, rather optimistically, as 'bullet proof' glass).

In several fighter designs the fuel tanks were situated underneath or

behind the pilot; since the fuel provided an excellent medium to slow bullets, the tanks protected whatever was behind them. The strength of the argument for this did weaken, however, if the tank itself burst into flames on being hit and roasted the pilot! In the majority of cases where fuel fires were started as a result of enemy action, the wall of the tank had first been punctured and the fuel had caught fire when it was *outside* the tank. So if full armour protection for the tanks was going to be prohibitively heavy, the next best thing was to prevent fuel from leaking out of tanks that had been hit. The solution most generally employed involved the use of a layer of uncured rubber round the outside of the tank. When a bullet struck the tank it passed clean through the layer and the wall of the tank and into the fuel; but when the fuel began to pour out of the hole it caused a chemical reaction with the rubber, which then swelled up and sealed off the hole.

In addition to self-sealing tanks similar to those described above, the Russians fitted several of their fighters with a system whereby carbon dioxide and nitrogen from the engine exhaust gases were passed, via coolers and filters, into the fuel tanks. By thus substituting inert gases for the potentially explosive fuel-air mixture in partially emptied or empty tanks, the chances of fuel fires were greatly reduced. When they finally saw the light and began protecting their fighters, late in the war, the Japanese employed a similar system using carbon dioxide from bottles.

For his direct protection, the fighter pilot was usually provided with steel armour plates of up to 13 mm thick, disposed behind his head and body and in strategic positions about the aircraft. One of the most heavily protected fighters of the Second World War was the U.S. Navy's F6F Hellcat, which carried a total of 456 pounds of armour plate, toughened glass, Duralamin deflector plates and self-sealing material for the fuel tanks.

During the early part of the war several fighter types were hastily modified to carry armour and toughened glass protection for the pilot. Such piecemeal improvements could bring problems of their own, however, as in the case of the P-39 Airacobra whose toughened glass windscreen had a thick frame which restricted forward visibility. In the centre of the windscreen was the S.T. 1A reflector sight.

Layout of F6F Hellcat.

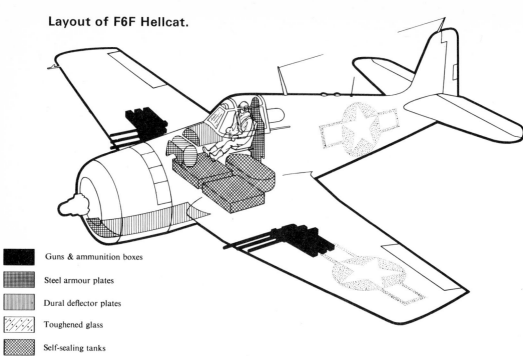

■ Guns & ammunition boxes

▦ Steel armour plates

▥ Dural deflector plates

▨ Toughened glass

▦ Self-sealing tanks

▤ Oil tanks

The layout of this protection is shown in the diagram above. One interesting idea confined to German and Russian aircraft was the substitution of the steel plate immediately behind the pilot's head with a panel of toughened glass 70 mm to 90 mm thick; in this way the pilot was given a measure of protection without restricting his rearward vision.

By the end of the war, in addition to those mentioned above, the following steps were taken at the design stage to reduce the vulnerability of

An interesting idea fitted to many German and Russian fighters, in this case a Russian Yak-3, was a toughened glass shield behind the pilot's head; this provided him with protection almost as good as that from steel plate, but without restricting his vision rearwards. *via Icare*

The layout of the Yak-3

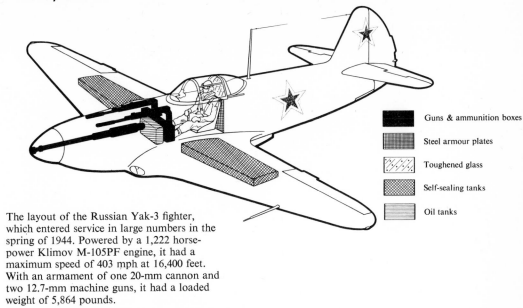

Guns & ammunition boxes	
Steel armour plates	
Toughened glass	
Self-sealing tanks	
Oil tanks	

The layout of the Russian Yak-3 fighter, which entered service in large numbers in the spring of 1944. Powered by a 1,222 horsepower Klimov M-105PF engine, it had a maximum speed of 403 mph at 16,400 feet. With an armament of one 20-mm cannon and two 12.7-mm machine guns, it had a loaded weight of 5,864 pounds.

fighters: the use of electrical systems wherever possible in preference to hydraulic systems, whose oil constituted a fire risk; where hydraulic systems were used, their oil piping had to be kept as short as possible; and the location of fuel, oil, hydraulic and oxygen piping and electrical and control wiring as far as possible from the outer skin of the aircraft, so that they received a measure of protection from the structure. The last of these measures did, of course, run directly contrary to the requirement for easy maintenance. But who said fighter design was easy?

On the subject of fighter vulnerability, an interesting point to consider is the degree by which this was increased by the carriage of fuel in non-self-sealing drop tanks. Firing trials carried out in the U.S.A. late in the war showed that even in extreme cases, where the drop tanks were hit and blew open, the fuel fell clear downwards and no trailing fire resulted; exploding drop tanks showed no tendency to fragment, rather they split into large pieces which moved outwards at low velocity and caused little secondary damage. Since fire cannot exist without a plentiful supply of oxygen, the flames from a burning tank could not possibly creep up fuel lines and reach other tanks inside the aircraft. The trial showed that in most cases the only effect of the drop tank being hit while in place was that it absorbed a blow which the aircraft would otherwise have had to take. From all of this a general conclusion was reached: it was unnecessary for a fighter pilot to jettison his tanks unless he really needed the extra performance which resulted; even if he was surprised by an enemy and hit in the drop tank, almost invariably the latter could be released before it caused damage. It was an important finding, particularly for those responsible for planning operations from aircraft carriers where storage space for expendable items was always at a premium.

Again and again fighters demonstrated that they could return to base with quite major structural damage; this P-47 of the 318th Fighter Group, U.S.A.A.F., came back after an explosive shell had blown a hole clean through the starboard wing and removed a large section of skin from the underside. *U.S.A.A.F.*

One of the most detailed sources of information on the relative causes of aircraft losses is from a U.S. Navy survey of aircraft lost or damaged by Japanese air-to-air action between September 1944 and August 1945. The 501 single-engined aircraft considered in the survey include torpedo bombers and dive bombers as well as fighters; but since all were of similar layout and construction, the figures are relevant to this account.

Position of Hit	Total Number of Aircraft Hit	Number of Aircraft Lost	Percentage Loss of Aircraft Hit
Propeller	9	0	0
Power Plant	37	23	62
Structure	215	23	11
Pilot and/or Controls	97	74	76
Control Surfaces	27	0	0
Oil System	27	23	85
Fuel System	30	24	80
Hydraulic System	35	21	60
Electrical System	6	0	0
Others	18	5	28
	501	193	38

These statistics require some qualification before they can be considered representative for all fighters. Throughout the survey, a lost aircraft was defined as one that had failed to return to a friendly base after being hit; a damaged aircraft was one that had returned to base after being hit, whether it was repairable or not. All of the U.S. Navy aircraft in the sample were powered by air-cooled engines; had these aircraft been fitted with liquid-cooled engines almost all of those hit in the engine (or its associated cooling system) would have been lost. It is likely that the number of pilots hit was greater than the figures would suggest, since those aircraft that went missing without trace were not included.

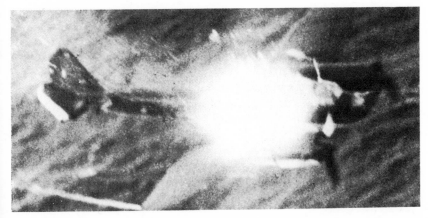

Once fire had broken out, the chances of survival for an aircraft were slim. This Junkers 88 crashed shortly after this picture was taken, following a brush with Mosquito fighters off Norway in November 1943. *I.W.M.*

Certain interesting facts emerge from the table. The first is the extreme vulnerability of even an air-cooled engine; only 38 per cent of the aircraft were able to survive damage in that area. Similarly there was the vulnerability of the fuel and oil systems, with only a 15 to 20 per cent chance of survival of damage to these *in spite of the use of self-sealing tanks in all aircraft*. Damage to the hydraulic system was also a significant cause of losses, with only a 40 per cent chance of survival. In these three cases the damage usually resulted in a fuel or oil fire, and it was this that caused the loss of the aircraft (in a similar survey of fighter losses carried out by the U.S.A.A.F., fire occurred in 59 per cent of the cases, and there was smoke in an additional 13 per cent). In spite of the armour and other protection round the cockpit – and the U.S. Navy was second to none when it came to providing this – more than a third of the aircraft lost had suffered hits on the pilot or controls; and, as has been said, it is likely that an even greater proportion of the actual losses were due to this cause. On the other hand, the 89 per cent chance of an aircraft being able to survive hits on its structure indicates that this was one of the least vulnerable parts of a fighter.

The Power to Fight

The question of which was the better type of engine for a fighter, the liquid-cooled in-line or the air-cooled radial, was the subject of considerable discussion both before and during the war. On the matter of aerodynamic cleanliness the in-line won easily; it had, as one in-line devotee put it, its cylinders in neat lines compared with those of the radial which were 'spread about like the leaves of a cabbage'. At the beginning of the war in-line engines were being built with a frontal area of just under one square inch for each horse-power they developed, compared with two-and-a-half times this figure for the radial; by the end of the conflict the in-line engines existed with a frontal area of under half a square inch per horse-power, with the best radial engines less than three-quarters more than this. Water cooling was the more efficient method, because it was a comparatively simple matter to duct the coolant to the hot points of the engine where it was required and achieve an even degree of cooling; air-cooled engines had to rely on fins and baffles and the result was less satisfactory. On the other hand the supporters of the radial could argue that their engine was the lighter; at the beginning of the war a 1,000 horse-power radial weighed about 100 pounds less than an in-line of similar power, and this did not include the extra weight of the cooling liquid, the radiators and all the associated plumbing. In action the cooling system of in-line engines proved extremely vulnerable to battle damage, and even a small hole in the piping or radiator was sufficient to allow the coolant to escape and bring the engine to a steaming halt; in general, radial engines were only about half as vulnerable to battle damage as were in-line engines.

During the Second World War fighter designers were almost evenly divided on the relative merits of the two types of engine, with the liquid-cooled in-line gaining the edge in popularity for the final generation of piston-engined types under development at the end of the conflict.

We have observed how the designers of fighter airframes achieved a wide measure of agreement on the best layout to use for this role. In contrast, the engine manufacturers each seemed to pick on a type of motor and one or more form of power boosting, and stick with it and make it work.

Pre-eminent amongst in-line engines during the Second World War was the Rolls-Royce Merlin, a 27-litre V-12 which was built in many thousands in Great Britain and under licence by Packard in the U.S.A. A sound engine at the beginning of the war, the Merlin was developed to the last ounce of its capability before the end. In essence, the story of the development of the Merlin centred on the fitting of progressively more powerful superchargers. The power produced by a piston engine, like that from a turbo-jet, is directly related to the amount of air passing through it in a given time; the greater the mass flow of air, the greater the power developed. Since for a given piston engine the capacity of the cylinders was fixed, and there were mechanical constraints which limited the rotational speed of the components, one obvious way to increase the power was to increase the compression ratio of the supercharger so that it squeezed a greater mass of air into the cylinders. By means of design refinements and the use of higher octane fuels, the resultant cooling and detonation* problems could be kept within bounds.

Half way through the war Rolls-Royce introduced the Mark 61 Merlin, which featured a two-stage supercharger with two centrifugal compressors in series. However, by the time it had passed through both supercharger stages the charge was very hot indeed and likely to detonate in the cylinders. To overcome this problem Rolls-Royce engineers developed the inter-cooler, a rather clever radiator-in-reverse which cooled the charge and made it possible to use higher compression ratios without risk of detonation.

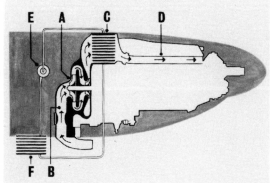

E Water pump
A Supercharger impellers
C Intercooler
D Induction pipe to cylinders
F Radiator
B Fuel and air mixture

Arrangement of the two-stage supercharger and intercooler, fitted to the Merlin 61 engine.

*Detonation. When an engine is working normally, the charge in the cylinder is ignited by the spark and progressive burning takes place giving a controlled push on the piston. But as the pressure and temperature of the charge are increased by supercharging there comes a time when, after ignition by the spark, the charge burns progressively but before the burning is complete the unburnt portion of the charge reaches a pressure and a temperature high enough to cause it to ignite spontaneously. This occurs with an explosive 'pinking' noise, familiar to motorists though not audible in an aircraft due to the propeller and other noises. The resultant detonation subjects the piston to a hammer blow rather than a push causing a loss of efficiency and, if severe and prolonged, will cause all sorts of damage to the engine. One way to raise the threshold of detonation is to use a fuel of a higher octane value.

The Rolls-Royce Merlin 45 engine, fitted to the Mark V Spitfire, developed 1,470 horse-power for a weight of 1,385 pounds. *I.W.M.*

The Rolls-Royce Griffon 61, fitted to the Mark XIV Spitfire, developed 2,035 horse-power for a weight of 2,090 pounds. By repositioning some of the components in the engine bay of the Spitfire, notably the oil tank from the underside of the engine to behind it, it was possible to fit the Griffon into a space little greater than that occupied by the Merlin. *Costain*

By the use of such methods, the power obtained from the Merlin was increased by leaps and bounds. The Merlin III fitted to the Spitfire I in 1939 developed 1,030 horse-power, using 87 octane fuel. By mid-1944 the Merlin 130 series of engines fitted to the Hornet, with the same 27-litre capacity but with two-stage supercharging and burning 100/150 octane fuel, was delivering 2,030 horse-power. This represented an increase in power of almost as much again and was a magnificent technical achievement.

After the Merlin had proved itself Rolls-Royce engineers began work on its heavier successor, the Griffon. Although this engine had a capacity of 36 litres (which was a third greater than that of the Merlin), by some inspired juggling of the camshaft and magneto drives its designers managed to keep the frontal area of the Griffon to within six per cent, and the length to within three inches, of the earlier engine; more to the point, the Griffon weighed only a few hundred pounds more than the Merlin and could be fitted into many of the airframes originally designed for the smaller engine. The Griffon 61, which powered the Spitfire XIV which entered service in 1944, developed 2,035 horse-power using normal 100/130 octane fuel.

The other important in-line engine fitted to British fighters was the Napier Sabre, a 36.6-litre job with twenty-four cylinders in an H-layout. Amongst the unusual features of this engine was the use of sleeve valves instead of the usual poppet valves. As well as being somewhat lighter, the former made detonation less likely and so a higher compression ratio could be used with a fuel of a given octane rating. The disadvantage of the sleeve valve was that it acted like an overcoat round the piston and made cooling difficult, though after a bit of a struggle Napier engineers were able to reduce the problem to manageable proportions. With single stage supercharging the Sabre IIB developed 2,400 horse-power to power the Tempest V. Before the war ended the Sabre VII was running at 3,055 horse-power and was capable of more, but the conflict was over before this engine could be used operationally.

Engine mechanics using a hand crank to start the Daimler-Benz DB 601A engine of a Messerschmitt 109E. This twelve cylinder inverted 'V' developed 1,100 horse-power.

In Germany the Daimler-Benz company started the war with its 33.9-litre DB 601 engine, developing 1,100 horse-power. We have observed that this engine was broadly comparable to the early Merlin III. But from there the Daimler-Benz engineers did not take the same development road as their counterparts at Rolls-Royce; instead of trying to drag the last ounce of power out of their engine they brought out two new ones based on it, the DB 603 and the DB 605. The DB 603 had a capacity of 44.5 litres and initially developed 1,750 horse-power. The DB 605 was not quite so large, with a capacity of only 35.7 litres and an output of 1,475 horse-power. And when they developed these engines the Germans did not go straight to two-stage supercharging but instead preferred to use water-methanol or nitrous oxide injection to increase power for short periods.

Water-methanol injection (code-named MW-30 or MW-50 depending upon whether 30 or 50 per cent methanol was used in the mixture) improved performance at altitudes *below* the rated altitude* of the engine. The water did the work; the methanol was there merely to prevent the water freezing at low temperatures. The mixture was injected into the eye of the supercharger and acted as an anti-detonant, cooling the charge and enabling higher compression ratios to be used. Applied to the DB 605 engine of the Messerschmitt 109G, MW-50 injection at approximately half a gallon per minute increased power by between 120 and 150 horse-power at sea level for a maximum period of 10 minutes.

Nitrous oxide injection (code-named GM-1) was used to improve the performance *above* the rated altitude of the engine. The nitrous oxide (laughing gas) was stored at minus 88 degrees centigrade in its liquid form in heavily lagged containers. It was injected into the supercharger inlet, where it provided additional oxygen for combustion, acted as an anti-detonant and cooled the charge; its effect was to enable the engine to

*Rated Altitude. The altitude at which the supercharger is allowed to deliver its full pressure to the induction manifold. Above the rated altitude, the power delivered by a supercharged piston engine gradually decreases.

continue to deliver high power at greater altitudes than would otherwise have been the case. The DB 605 DCM fitted in the Messerschmitt 109K carried both MW-50 and GM-1 boosting. The effect of the latter on altitude performance may be seen from the following official figures: maximum power at 19,600 feet rated altitude, 1,550 horse-power (above this level the power output normally would begin to fall steadily); maximum power at 27,800 feet, with nitrous oxygen injected at 8 pounds per minute, 1,350 horse-power; maximum power at 32,800 feet, with nitrous oxide injected at 16 pounds per minute, 1,350 horse-power.

The two injection systems did, however, carry with them weight penalties. The MW-50 installation for the Messerschmitt 190G-14 weighed about 300 pounds, complete with 26 gallons of water-methanol. The GM-1 installation fitted to some versions of the Messerschmitt 109G weighed about 670 pounds, with 16 gallons of nitrous oxide. 'Right thinking' Rolls-Royce engineers would argue that having containers of various odd concoctions, with pipes running all over the place, was a poor substitute for a supercharger of the correct capacity. On the other hand the Germans had no fancy high octane fuels on which to run highly supercharged engines on the Rolls-Royce pattern; they had to do the best they could using fuels of 100 octane rating and lower.

During the final year of the war the Junkers company's Jumo 213 engine of almost 35-litre capacity went into service in the potent D model of the Focke Wulf 190. Although it was a 12-cylinder inverted V in-line in the typical German mould, in the Fw 190D the engine looked at first glance like the radial engine it replaced; this was because the designer Kurt Tank had installed the radiator immediately in front of the liquid-cooled in-line engine, thus effectively removing the former from the projected frontal area of the aircraft and reducing overall drag. It is remarkable that no other operational single-engined fighter type during the Second World War employed this fundamentally neat system, for it was by no means novel: it had been employed during the First World War on

Although at first sight it appears to be powered by a radial engine, the Focke Wulf 190D was in fact fitted with a 2,240 horse-power Jumo 213 liquid cooled in-line with an annular radiator. This fighter had a maximum speed of 426 mph at 21,500 feet; it carried an armament of two 20-mm cannon and two 13-mm machine guns, and had a loaded weight of 9,480 pounds.

Close-up of the Jumo 213 installation in the Focke Wulf 190D, showing the neat arrangement of the engine bearers and the accessibility of the sparking plugs and ignition system. *Focke Wulf*

several types including the British SE 5 and the German Fokker D-7, and from the beginning of the Second World War on the German Junkers 88 twin-engined bomber and long range fighter.

The Jumo 213 underwent much the same sort of development as the Daimler-Benz fighter engines, with nitrous oxide and water-methanol used to boost its power. For one of the final variants of the Focke Wulf 190 family, the Ta 152H, Junkers engineers used every trick in the book to boost high altitude performance: the Jumo 213E which powered this aircraft featured both two-stage supercharging *and* nitrous oxide injection. The engine developed 1,750 horse-power for take-off; at 35,400 feet it developed 1,310 horse-power or, with nitrous oxide injection at 13.5 pounds per minute, a very respectable 1,730 horse-power. The Ta 152H was credited with a maximum speed of 472 mph at 41,000 feet, a remarkable performance which came close to the limits of what was possible using a piston engine.

The only in-line engine of indigenous design to enter large-scale production for fighters in the U.S.A. during the war was the Allison V-1710, a 28-litre V-12. It proved to be an unreliable engine in service, however, and was scarcely in the same league as the Merlin which replaced it in the P-51 to make that fighter one of the all-time greats. Technically the V-1710's claim to fame must rest on its being the first engine with turbo-supercharging to become operational in a fighter, the P-38 Lightning. The idea of using the engine exhaust gases to drive a turbine, which in turn drove a supercharger, had about it an air of getting something for nothing. Moreover the higher the aircraft flew the greater was the pressure differential between the exhaust gases and the outside air, with the result that the turbo-supercharger ran fastest when it was most needed, at high altitude. The turbo-supercharger did, however, pose problems of its own.

The principal difficulty was metallurgical: the turbine had to run at red heat, in the region of 600 to 800 degrees centigrade; add to this a rotational speed of 22,000 rpm or more, and it can be seen that specialised materials were necessary if the blades were to survive this sort of treatment. Only the American General Electric Company, a firm with considerable experience in building high temperature steam turbines, was able to bring a successful turbo-supercharger into large scale production. But getting the turbo-supercharger to work was one thing, getting it into a fighter was another. The fighters that carried the device had almost to be built round it. In the case of the Lightning fighter, the twin-boom layout was selected because the booms presented a convenient housing for the engines and their associated turbo-superchargers. Not the least remarkable feature of the early models of the Lightning was the manner in which the compressed air from the turbo-supercharger was cooled before it was passed to the second-stage, engine driven, supercharger fitted to the V-1710: the air was ducted along the leading edge of each wing from boom to tip and back again, providing wing anti-icing as a useful bonus. It was an arrangement that sacrificed too much to the dictates of aerodynamic cleanliness, however, and on the later versions of the Lightning it was replaced by a more conventional intercooler using a radiator on the front of the engine.

At the beginning of the war the French in-line fighters were all powered by the 35-litre Hispano 12Y, a rugged engine whose development virtually ceased in its country of origin with the armistice. However, this engine was already in licence production in Russia as the Klimov M-100 and was later developed into the M-103, M-105 and M-107 engines which powered all the Soviet in-line engined fighters of the late war period. With a two-speed supercharger the M-107 developed 1,650 horse-power for take-off, with a power-to-weight ratio up to the best western designs. The engine was good

Engine maintenance in the open for Yak-1M fighters of the Soviet Air Force. The 1,100 horse-power Klimov M-105 engine fitted to this aircraft was developed from the French Hispano 12Y; on its power the Yak-1M reached a speed of 364 mph at 16,400 feet. This fighter carried an armament of one 20-mm cannon and two 7.62-mm machine guns, and had a loaded weight of 6,217 pounds. During operations under extreme winter conditions, it was the practice in the Soviet Air Force to drain the engine oil and coolant tanks after each flight, and prior to engine starting re-fill them with warmed fluids. *via Icare.*

The Italians lacked a suitable in-line engine for their fighters and licence-produced the Daimler-Benz 601 as the Alfa Romeo Monsoni; its 1,175 horse-power gave the Macchi 202 (illustrated) a maximum speed of 370 mph at 16,400 feet. This fighter, which entered service during the summer of 1941, carried an armament of two 12.7-mm and two 7.9-mm machine guns, and its loaded weight was 6,459 pounds.

Also lacking a suitable in-line engine for their fighters, the Japanese too bought the Daimler-Benz DB 601 and from it developed the 1,175 horse-power Kawasaki Ha 40. Its power gave the Army's Kawasaki Ki 61-I (illustrated), which entered service in the spring of 1943, a maximum speed of 348 mph at 16,400 feet. This fighter (code-named 'Tony' by the Allies) carried an armament of two 20-mm cannon and two 12.7-mm machine guns, and had a loaded weight of 7,650 pounds.

enough to take the Yak-9U to 415 mph at 16,000 feet, and made it a formidable opponent for its German counterparts. Perhaps surprisingly, in view of the assembly and maintenance problems associated with it and the unkind remarks often made about pre-1945 Russian technology, most Russian fighters had direct fuel injection by the end of the war.

Neither the Italians nor the Japanese succeeded in getting an in-line engine of their own design into large scale production for fighters during the war. Both made up for this deficiency by producing German Daimler-Benz designs under licence. In Italy the DB 601 was built by Alfa Romeo as the Monsoni and the DB 605 was built by Fiat as the Tifone. In Japan Kawasaki produced derivatives of the DB 601.

So much for the in-line engines fitted to fighters. Pre-eminent amongst

Ground crewmen working on the Pratt and Whitney R-2800-59 engine which developed 2,300 horse-power for the P-47C Thunderbolt. Under the rear of the engine can be seen the huge duct for the carburettor air; this ran almost the length of the fuselage, to the turbo-supercharger in the rear. *via Holmes*

radial engines for this purpose was the American Pratt and Whitney R-2800 Double Wasp, a huge 45.9-litre creation with eighteen cylinders in two rows and employing direct· fuel injection. Developing 2,000 horse-power for take-off, the Double Wasp powered the P-47 Thunderbolt for the U.S.A.A.F. and the F4U Corsair, the F6F Hellcat, the F7F Tigercat and the F8F Bearcat designs for the U.S. Navy. Getting rid of the excess heat is always a problem with a radial engine, especially when that radial is subjected to the stress of fighter operations. The most difficult part to cool is the exhaust valve, and the Pratt and Whitney engineers solved this problem by using hollow mushroom-headed valves partially filled with sodium to help conduct away the heat. In the Hellcat the Double Wasp was fitted with two-stage supercharging and water-methanol injection; the

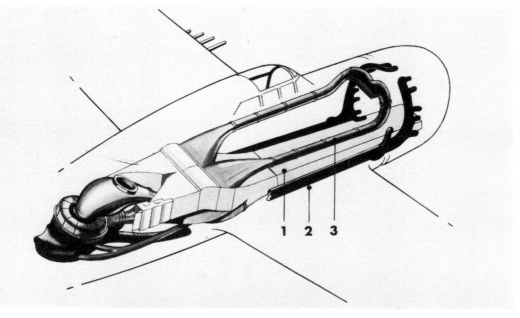

The main reason why the P-47 Thunderbolt was such a large aircraft was that its fuselage had to house some 60 feet of air ducting between the engine in the nose and the turbo-supercharger in the rear.

1 Air from intake
2 Exhaust gases to drive turbo-supercharger
3 Compressed air from turbo-supercharger

use of the latter gave the aircraft an additional 20 mph in horizontal speed and an increase in the rate of climb of 650 feet per minute, up to the rated altitude of 18,000 feet.

We have observed that the use of turbo-superchargers dictated the twin-boom layout of the P-38 Lightning. The use of the device had a similar coercive effect on the internal layout of the P-47 Thunderbolt, for weight and space considerations necessitated the fitting of the turbo-supercharger in the rear fuselage. As a result the carburettor air was collected through an inlet at the base of the engine in the nose and carried back some *twenty feet* to the turbo-supercharger then, after compression, *twenty feet* forwards to the mechanically-driven second-stage supercharger on the rear of the engine; when this air emerged from the engine as exhaust gas, it was ducted a further *twenty feet* back to the turbine of the turbo-supercharger before it was exhaled. This meant ducting on a large scale; for the compressed air it meant high pressure ducting and for the exhaust gases it meant very hot ducting with sliding joints to allow for the expansion of the metal. With so much air being pushed around inside it, it is hardly surprising that with the Double Wasp at the front, a tank for 256 Imp (305 U.S.) gallons of fuel in the middle and the turbo-supercharger at the rear, the fuselage of the Thunderbolt was just plain huge. That the aircraft went into service at all as a fighter is surprising; that it proved successful, with a magnificent reputation for surviving battle damage, is

little short of amazing. Ironically, in view of the trouble designer Alexander Kartveli had gone to in order to produce a high altitude fighter, the Thunderbolt was to achieve its greatest success at low altitude as a fighter bomber – where it could easily have done without the turbo-supercharger and all that bulky ducting.

After the Americans, in terms of the number of fighters produced with radial engines, the Japanese came next as exponents of this type of motor. At the beginning of the war in the Pacific the most important radials in production for fighters were the fourteen-cylinder Nakajima types for the Army Ki 43 (Oscar) and the Navy A6M2 (Zero); these engines were fitted with single-speed superchargers, and were in the 1,000 horse-power class. Shortly afterwards Mitsubishi introduced its Kasei series of fourteen cylinder engines which, with a two-speed supercharger, developed 1,360 horse-power at 15,000 feet. By the early part of 1943 the Kasei had been further improved, and the Nakajima engines fitted with two-speed superchargers, to improve performance at altitudes around 20,000 feet. Also at this time Nakajima introduced its new eighteen cylinder Homare engine of 32 litres capacity which, with water-methanol injection, developed a fraction under 2,000 horse-power for take-off. During the closing stages of the war the Japanese were struggling to get into service fighters with engines developing up to 2,200 horse-power, some of them with turbo-superchargers; but they did not quite manage it before the surrender.

In 1939 the bulk of the Russian fighter force was equipped with the Polikarpov I-16; in its many variants this fighter was powered by the M-25, the M-62 or the M-63 nine cylinder radial of 28.9 litres capacity, developed from the American Wright Cyclone. The path of improvement followed that taken in other countries with first single-speed then two-speed superchargers and higher compression ratios with higher octane fuels; by these means the power output was increased from 725 horse-power from the M-25 to 1,000 horse-power for the M-62 and M-63. During 1941 the fourteen cylinder 41.2-litre Schvetsov M-82 went into production, which

The P-47D Thunderbolt, showing the bubble-type canopy which provided the pilot with a better view to the rear and which became fashionable for fighters during the latter part of the war. Powered by a R-2800-59 developing 2,535 horse-power, this version of the P-47 had a maximum speed of 433 mph at 30,000 feet, carried an armament of six or eight .5-inch machine guns, and loaded weighed 13,500 pounds. *U.S.A.A.F.*

When it entered
service early in 1944
the Kawanishi N1K1
(Allied code-name
'George 11') was one
of the most potent
fighters operated by
the Japanese Navy.
Powered by a 1,990
horse-power
Nakajima Homare 21
engine, it had a
maximum speed of
362 mph at 17,700
feet. It carried an
armament of four 20-
mm cannon and two
7.7-mm machine
guns, and loaded
weighed 9,526 pounds.
U.S.N

also owed much to Wright practice. Initially this engine developed 1,570 horse-power, later increased to 1,870 horse-power; these engines powered the successful Lavochkin series of radial engined fighters.

In Germany the only radial engine to go into large-scale production for fighters was the BMW 801, a fourteen cylinder 41.8-litre engine which powered the Focke Wulf 190A which came as such a nasty shock to the Royal Air Force during the autumn of 1941. The BMW 801 was a remarkably compact engine, with cooling assisted by a twelve-bladed fan fitted to its front. With a two-speed supercharger the BMW 801 developed 1,600 horse-power for take-off and 1,440 horse-power at 18,700 feet; this was soon raised to 1,700 horse-power for take-off and later, with water-methanol injection, to 1,790 horse-power for short bursts. In spite of its initial success as a fighter engine the BMW 801 underwent comparatively little development and was replaced in the Fw 190 fighters (though not in the fighter bomber variants) late in the war by the in-line Jumo 213.

With world-beating in-line engines such as the Merlin, the Griffon and the Sabre in large scale production, British designers had little inclination or need to fit radial engines into their fighters. The exceptions to this general rule were the twin-engined Blenheim and Beaufighter aircraft, powered by Bristol Mercury and Hercules engines respectively, and the single-engined Mark II Tempest at the very end of the war with the Bristol Centaurus. The Mercury was a very ordinary nine cylinder 24.9-litre design developing 840 horse-power and was already obsolescent as a power plant for fighters at the beginning of the war. The Hercules was a modern fourteen cylinder 38.7-litre engine with sleeve valves which, with the provision of single-speed then two-speed supercharging, worked its way from 1,325 horse-power to over 1,800 horse-power; it was a huge success powering heavy aircraft, but its use in the Beaufighter probably owed much to the fact that Bristols made the aircraft as well as the engine. Be that as it may Bristol's successor to the Hercules, the colossal 53.6-litre eighteen cylinder Centaurus, which developed 2,400 horse-power for a later version of the Tempest, could stand on its own feet as a fighter engine.

Italian and French radial engine development can be summed up in a few lines. In 1939 the Italian fighters in large-scale production, the biplane Fiat CR 42 and the monoplane Fiat G.50 and Macchi C.200, were powered by the outdated Fiat A.74 fourteen cylinder radial which developed a good deal less than 900 horse-power. Clearly this was not good enough, and although better radials were in the pipeline the Italians switched to using licence-built Daimler-Benz in-lines for their fighters. At the beginning of the war the French possessed a good developed radial in the Gnôme Rhône 14, which produced 1,100 horse-power for the Bloch 152 fighter and later, in the much-modified 14R version, 1,580 horse-power; but the latter engine was too late to enter service before the armistice.

Enter the Jet

Before discussing the relative merits of piston engine and jet propulsion, it is important to appreciate the different relationship between forward speed and thrust for each. In the case of the piston engine, the rotational power has to be converted by the propeller into thrust, to drive the aircraft; but the faster the aircraft flies, the lower is the efficiency of the propeller.

Opposite:

Close-up of the compact installation of the BMW 801 fourteen cylinder radial, fitted to the Focke Wulf 190A. Protruding from the cowling above the rear of the engine may be seen the barrels of the two synchronised 7.9-mm machine guns.

The thrust from the jet engine, on the other hand, is produced directly and remains nearly constant throughout the speed range of the aircraft.

Consider the case of the Mark I Spitfire which, in round figures, had a maximum speed of 300 mph at sea level on an engine developing 1,000 horse-power. At this speed the propeller was about 80 per cent efficient, so the number of horse-power actually converted into thrust was about 800; it can be shown that this was equivalent to 1,000 pounds of thrust, and was approximately equal to the drag produced by the Mark I Spitfire at that speed. Thus, at 300 mph, one horse-power produced at the engine generated approximately one pound of thrust to drive the aircraft.

Now consider the amount of power needed to propel the same airframe at twice the speed, 600 mph. Drag increases with the square of the speed, so the effect of going twice as fast is to increase the drag by four times; thus 1,000 pounds of drag at 300 mph becomes 4,000 pounds of drag at 600 mph. (For simplicity, the possible increased drag due to compressibility at 600 mph has been omitted in this discussion.) To overcome this quadrupled drag it would be necessary to have an engine able to produce four times the thrust, 4,000 pounds. It can be shown that this was the equivalent of 6,400 horse-power converted into thrust. But at 600 mph the efficiency of the propeller was only about 53 per cent; so to drive the airframe at this speed it was necessary to have a piston engine developing not 6,400 but 12,000 horse-power. In 1945 the best piston engines weighed just under one pound for each horse power they produced, so a piston engine to push a Spitfire airframe to 600 mph would have weighed about 11,000 pounds – or about twice as much as the entire all-up weight of the early models of this aircraft! Even the early jet engines could do much better than this. The Walter 509A rocket fitted to the Messerschmitt 163 developed 3,750 pounds of thrust for an installed weight of 813 pounds; the two Jumo 004B engines which powered the Me 262 delivered a combined thrust of just under 4,000 pounds for a weight of 2,650 pounds. Before the end of the war the Rolls-Royce Nene was developing more than 4,000 pounds of thrust for a weight of less than 1,500 pounds.

The first operational use of jet propulsion was with the Walter 509A rocket motor which, as has been mentioned, powered the Me 163. It ran on two chemical fuels, code-named T Stoff and C Stoff by the Germans. T Stoff was the name given to highly-concentrated hydrogen peroxide, an unstable compound which was liable to decompose on contact with copper, lead, organic materials or any combustible; on decomposition it gave out heat at a rate equivalent to that of gunpowder. It was also highly corrosive, and not its least unendearing feature was that it would burn away human flesh if it was in contact for more than a few seconds. The Me 163 carried more than a ton and a half of this vile brew in three tanks, one on either side of the cockpit and one behind it, which can have done little for the pilot's peace of mind. The other fuel, C Stoff, was a combination of methyl alcohol, hydrazine hydrate and a little water. It was relatively stable unless by accident or design it came into contact with the T Stoff, in which case the latter went into its decomposing routine. The two fuels were brought together in the ratio of about three parts of T Stoff to one part of C Stoff in the combustion chamber of the rocket, where they reacted to produce a jet of nitrogen and superheated steam with a velocity of about 6,500 feet

per second and a temperature of 1,800 degrees centigrade. At its maximum thrust of 3,750 pounds the Walter 590A used about 20 pounds of fuel per second, which represented a rate of consumption per pound of thrust about *fifteen times* greater than that of an equivalent turbo-jet. The rocket motor endowed the Me 163 with a sparkling speed and climbing performance; but the instability of the T Stoff made its operation rather too exciting for general service use, and the type achieved little in action.

It soon became clear that the best way of providing jet propulsion for the new generation of fighters was the turbo-jet engine; during the latter half of the war work on such power units was accelerating in Great Britain and the U.S.A. on the one side, and in Germany and Japan on the other.

Just as there had been controversy over the relative merits of in-line or radial piston engines, so there were differences of opinion on the use of centrifugal or axial flow compressors for turbo-jets. In Britain and the U.S.A. the first turbo-jet engines to enter production employed the centrifugal compressor, which had the advantages of lightness, robustness and it was easy to manufacture. Both firms involved, Rolls-Royce and General Electric, had considerable experience in building centrifugal compressors for superchargers for piston engines; technically, it was a short step to build a similar but larger compressor on to the front of a jet engine. For reasons stated earlier, the Germans had not pushed the development of superchargers to the same pitch as had been the case in Britain and the U.S.A. So they did not lose much by going straight to what was basically the better type of compressor, the axial flow; the latter had the advantage that for a given compression ratio it had a somewhat smaller frontal area, though it was fragile and difficult to build into a mechanically reliable unit.

The results of the differing design philosophies in Britain and Germany can be seen from a comparison of the first turbo-jet engines to enter production: the Rolls-Royce Welland and the Junkers Jumo 004B. The Welland developed a thrust of 1,700 pounds for a diameter of 43 inches and a

Streaming nitrogen and superheated steam, a Messerschmitt 163 rocket fighter is seen accelerating away after take-off.

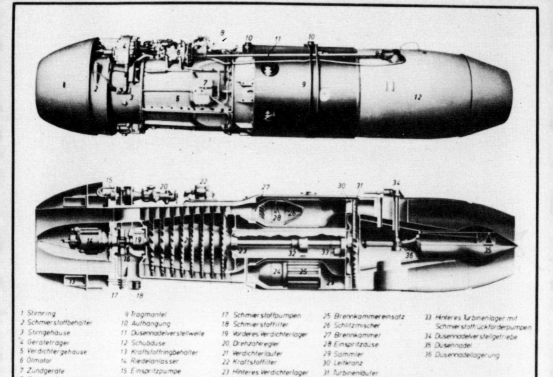

1 Stirnring	9 Tragmantel	17 Schmierstoffpumpen	25 Brennkammereinsatz	33 Hinteres Turbinenlager mit
2 Schmierstoffbehälter	10 Aufhängung	18 Schmierstoffilter	26 Schlitzmischer	Schmierstoffrückförderpumpen
3 Stirngehäuse	11 Düsennadelverstellwelle	19 Vorderes Verdichterlager	27 Brennkammer	34 Düsennadelverstellgetriebe
4 Gerätetrager	12 Schubdüse	20 Drehzahlregler	28 Einspritzdüse	35 Düsennadel
5 Verdichtergehäuse	13 Kraftstoffringbehälter	21 Verdichterläufer	29 Sammler	36 Düsennadellagerung
6 Ölmotor	14 Riedelanlasser	22 Kraftstoffilter	30 Leitkranz	
7 Zündgerate	15 Einspritzpumpe	23 Hinteres Verdichterlager	31 Turbinenläufer	
8 Bediengestangehebel	16 Abzweiggetriebe	24 Muffel	32 Vorderes Turbinenlager	

Stand Febr 44

Sondertriebwerk
Ansicht u. Schnitt

JFM 5450

Port side and sectioned views of the Junkers Jumo 004B, the first turbo-jet engine to go into large-scale production; it developed a thrust of 1,850 pounds, for a weight of about 1,600 pounds. 1. nose cowling. 2. oil tank. 3. entry casing. 4. auxiliary gear box. 5. compressor casing. 6. servo motor. 7. ignition box. 8. tail cone position control lever. 9. combustion chamber outer casing. 10. attachment points. 11. tail cone position control rod. 12. jet pipe. 13. annular fuel tank for starter motor. 14. starter motor. 15. fuel injection pump. 16. auxiliary drive. 17. oil pump. 18. oil filter. 19. front compressor bearing. 20. speed regulator. 21. axial flow compressor. 22. fuel filter. 23. rear compressor bearing. 24. flame tube. 25. combustion chamber muffle. 26. diffuser grill. 27. combustion chamber. 28. injection nozzle. 29. turbine entry ducting. 30. turbine stator blades. 31. turbine. 32. forward turbine bearing. 33. rear turbine bearing and oil scavenge pump. 34. movable tail cone operating gears. 35. movable tail cone. 36. tail cone support.

weight of about 850 pounds. The Jumo 004B developed 1,850 pounds of thrust for a diameter of 31.5 inches and a weight of about 1,590 pounds (the weight of some 004Bs could be greater by as much as 120 pounds, because to speed production the rough castings were machined only where absolutely necessary and there was a considerable variation in the sand moulds used). The eight-stage axial flow compressor of the 004B and the single-stage back-to-back centrifugal compressor of the Welland both gave compression ratios of about 3:1; but to achieve this the Welland had to run at a speed of 17,500 rpm, or about twice as fast as the 004B.

In terms of running life, the British and American turbo-jet engines were considerably better than those of the Germans. The latter were greatly handicapped by the shortages of chromium and nickel, which prevented the large scale use of high temperature alloys in Germany. In the absence of proper materials the combustion chambers of the 004B, for example, were made out of ordinary steel with a spray coating of aluminium baked on in an oven. It was a poor substitute and the theoretical 'life' of the combustion chambers was 25 running hours; in practice, it was frequently less. In contrast, the running life of similar components in British and American engines was about seven times as long; when it was declared suitable for service use in mid-1944, the Welland was cleared for 180 hours between overhauls.

Punch for the Fighter

As has been mentioned, in 1934 when the race began to develop fighters the usual armament was two slow-firing (about 750 rounds per minute) rifle-calibre machine guns. Obviously their weight of fire would be insufficient to knock down the sort of bombers to be expected at the end of the decade, and in each of the major nations work began on heavier armaments for fighters. By 1939 fighters were in service with three basic types of gun: the fast-firing rifle-calibre machine gun, the slower-firing heavy machine gun, and the shell-firing cannon.

At the outbreak of the Second World War all operational fighter aircraft carried rifle-calibre machine guns as all or part of their armament: the American Browning .300-inch (7.62 mm) or the similar licence-produced British .303-inch (7.7 mm), the French MAC 7.5-mm, the German Rheinmetall Borsig MG 17 of 7.9 mm, the Italian Breda SAFAT of 7.7 mm, the Polish Wzor of 7.7 mm, the Japanese Type 89 of 7.7 mm and the Russian ShKAS of 7.62 mm. Of these the ShKAS (*Shpitalny Komaritsky Aviatsionny Skorostrelny* – fast-firing aircraft gun) was, as has been mentioned, the best all-rounder; it had a rate of fire of 1,800 rounds per minute with a muzzle velocity of over 2,700 feet per second, all for a weight of 22 pounds.

Prior to the war three nations had put into service fighters equipped with .5-inch (12.7 mm) heavy machine guns: the U.S.A. with the .5 Browning, Italy with the 12.7-mm Breda SAFAT and Russia with the 12.7-mm UBS. Of these the Russian weapon was again the best. The UBS (*Universalny Berezina Skorostrelny* – Berezina universal fast-firing gun) had a rate of fire of 900 rounds per minute with a muzzle velocity of over 2,800 feet per second, for a weight of just over 47 pounds.

Fighter Fire Power 1939. The figures give the approximate weight of shells and projectiles that could be fired in a three-second burst (in action it was rare for a pilot to be able to hold his aim for longer); the figures are approximate because of the rate of fire of guns of the same type could vary by as much as 10 per cent. In the diagram each 'shell' represents a projectile weight of two pounds.

1. PZL-11c (Poland), four 7.7-mm machine guns, five pounds. 2. Curtiss P-36C (U.S.A.), one .5-inch (12.7 mm) and three .3-inch (7.62 mm) machine guns, seven pounds. 3. Supermarine Spitfire I (Great Britain), eight .303-inch (7.7 mm) machine guns, ten pounds. 4. Morane 406 (France), one 20-mm cannon and two 7.5-mm machine guns, twelve pounds. 5. Messerschmitt 109E (Germany), two 20-mm cannon and two 7.9-mm machine guns, thirteen pounds. 6. Messerschmitt 110C (Germany), two 20-mm cannon and four 7.9-mm machine guns, sixteen pounds. 7. Polikarpov I-16 (U.S.S.R.), two 20-mm cannon and two 7.62 machine guns, twenty-eight pounds.

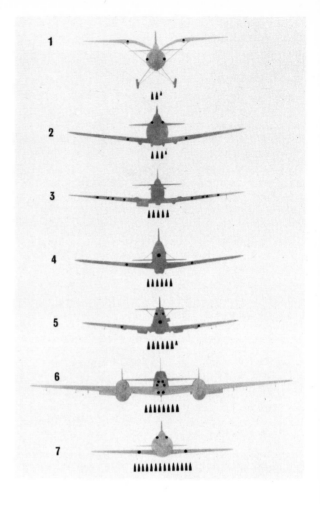

1 shell equals 2 pounds fired in 3 second burst

Finally there were the shell-firing cannon, of 20-mm calibre in each case (the arbitrary division between a machine gun and a cannon is that the latter has a calibre of 15 mm or greater). At the beginning of the war there were three types in service: the German Oerlikon, the French Hispano Suiza and the Russian ShVAK. Later the Oerlikon was manufactured under licence in Japan, and the Hispano was produced in Britain and, subsequently, in the U.S.A.

With a weight of only 60 pounds the Oerlikon MG FF was the lightest of the cannon, while the 4.7 ounce round it fired was the heaviest of the three. On the other hand its rate of fire of only 350 rounds per minute and its low muzzle velocity of 1,950 feet per second meant that the German weapon had the lowest performance in these respects. The Hispano Suiza cannon of the early war period was the heaviest of the weapons at 109 pounds; it fired 4.4 ounce rounds at a rate of 700 per minute and a muzzle

velocity of 2,820 feet per second, which meant that this weapon delivered a weight of fire about twice as great as that of the Oerlikon. The Russian ShVAK (*Shpitalny Vladimirov Aviatsionnaya Krupno Kalibernaya* – large calibre aircraft gun) was different again, with a weight of 92 pounds and firing light 3.5 ounce rounds at a rate of 800 per minute with a muzzle velocity of 2,820 feet per second. The Oerlikon and the early Hispano Suiza cannon were fed from drum magazines with a capacity of only 60 rounds; the ShVAK was belt fed.

During the first year of the war the trend was for aircraft to carry self-sealing tanks and armour protection for the crew positions, with the result that the effectiveness of fighters armed only with rifle-calibre machine guns was greatly reduced. The Royal Air Force had decided before the war that the Hispano Suiza was the best available cannon for use against armoured aircraft, as indeed it was. With its heavy projectile and very high

Armourers replenishing the ammunition boxes of the starboard wing battery of four .303-inch Browning machine guns of a Hurricane. Due to the difficulties of getting the Hispano cannon to work in such wing mountings, the eight .303-inch machine gun battery remained the standard armament for British single-engined fighters until well into 1941.
C. Brown

Typical .303-inch machine gun damage to a Heinkel 111; more than fifty hits are visible in this photograph. There are several well-authenticated accounts of German bombers having returned with more than two hundred hits from such rounds. By mid-1940 the general installation of armour plating and self-sealing fuel tanks had rendered the rifle calibre machine gun obsolescent as a bomber-destroying weapon.

muzzle velocity, the French cannon had a penetrative power about 50 per cent greater than the ShVAK and double that of the Oerlikon. During the summer of 1940 there was a struggle to get the Hispano operational in the Spitfires and Hurricanes. But the Hispano had originally been designed for mounting along the top of the engine of the fighter, so that the latter's weight could absorb the recoil forces; it did not take kindly to being pushed into less-rigid mountings out in the wings, which was the only place where there was room for it on the British single-engined fighters. The result was that the early service career of the Hispano in the Royal Air Force was a sad tale of frequent stoppages and failures, as the cannon tried to shake apart itself and its feed system during firing. When in the spring of 1941 the problems of the Hispano were finally sorted out, the Royal Air Force possessed a very reliable and hard-hitting weapon which was to serve it well for the remainder of the war.

In Germany the limitations of the Oerlikon were well appreciated before the war, but the weapon had to serve until the more effective Mauser MG 151/20 was ready for service. The Mauser 20-mm cannon had a rate of fire of 750 rounds per minute and a muzzle velocity of 2,500 feet per second. Like the Russian ShVAK it fired a 3.5 ounce shell, and it was broadly comparable in terms of weight and because it too used belt feeding. The Mauser weighed a bit less and fired a little bit faster than the Hispano, but its penetrative ability was considerably less.

Meanwhile, far away in the U.S.A., there had been a progressive up-gunning of the rather feebly armed fighters which had been in service in that country's air force at the beginning of the war. The armament fitted to new fighters moved up through various combinations of .3 and .5-inch machine guns and 20-mm and even 37-mm cannon, until by the early part of 1942 it began to settle down at four, six or eight .5-inch Browning heavy machine guns. Although the .5 Browning lacked the penetrative power of the 20-mm cannon the U.S. Army Ordnance department believed, rightly as it turned out, that this weapon would be perfectly adequate against the enemy aircraft likely to be encountered during the Second World War. The Germans never armoured their aircraft to withstand .5-inch rounds, and the Japanese certainly did not. But in case their hunch was wrong the Americans played it both ways and put the Hispano cannon into limited production; known as the M-2, the licence-built weapon was fitted into a small proportion of their fighters.

By the middle of the war all of the combatant nations had begun or completed the replacement of the rifle-calibre weapons in their fighters with cannon or heavy machine guns. The Japanese produced a near copy of the .5 Browning as the 12.7-mm Type 1 machine gun, with certain improvements over the original; the German Rheinmetall Borsig company produced the 13-mm MG 131 which fired a lighter round at a lower muzzle velocity than the Browning, though with a slightly higher rate of fire;

When the Hurricane Mark IIC armed with four 20-mm Hispano cannon entered service in the Royal Air Force in the spring of 1941, its weight of fire of 34 pounds in a three-second burst was greater than that of any other single-engined fighter in the world; moreover, the Hispano had the greatest armour-piercing capability of the 20-mm weapons to see service during the war. *C. Brown*

the Russians gradually replaced the rifle-calibre ShKAS gun with the UBS; and the Royal Air Force belatedly replaced the .303-inch machine gun in its Spitfires with .5 Brownings, when it was finally able to get hold of these precious weapons.

Against fighters or medium bombers carrying normal amounts of armour the fire power of the .5-inch heavy machine gun was adequate and that of the 20-mm cannon was ample. The trouble was, as the Germans and the Japanese began to discover from the latter half of 1942, that these weapons simply were not powerful enough against the tough American B-17 and B-24 heavy bombers. For example, the Focke Wulf 190A-3 carried an armament of two Oerlikon MG FF and two Mauser MG 151/20 20-mm cannon, and two rifle-calibre machine guns; during a three second burst these guns loosed off 130 rounds each of 20-mm and 7.9-mm ammunition. On the *average*, twenty hits of 20-mm were required to bring down one of the American heavy bombers;* unless they scored a lucky hit on the pilot or some other vital part, the rifle-calibre weapons were of little value in such an engagement. During the analysis of air-to-air combat films, armament experts found that the *average* Luftwaffe fighter pilot was hitting the bombers with only about *two per cent* of the aimed rounds that were fired. Thus, to obtain the twenty hits required to shoot down the heavy bomber, *one thousand rounds* of 20-mm ammunition had to be aimed at it; this represented twenty-three seconds firing time for the Fw 190A-3, an impossibly long time if the bomber was still in formation and the fighter pilot was himself on the receiving end of heavy defensive fire. It was found that the majority of the heavy bombers shot down by fighters fell either to the aces, who were beating the odds and getting far more than two per cent of their rounds on the target, or else the bombers were first damaged during previous fighter attacks or from flak and were forced out of formation, then finished off in long firing passes pressed home to short range.

Dr Samuel Johnson once assured us that when a man knows he is to be hanged in a fortnight it concentrates his mind beautifully. By the autumn of 1942 the Luftwaffe High Command knew that unless something was done soon they faced the prospect of having to meet large-scale daylight attacks on the German homeland, without adequately armed fighters. And the thought of that concentrated *their* minds beautifully.

Fortunately for the Luftwaffe, at this time the Rheinmetall Borsig company had two 30-mm heavy cannon in an advanced state of development and one of these, the MK 108, was chosen as the standard bomber destroying weapon. The MK 108 had a high rate of fire of 660 rounds per minute, though its muzzle velocity was only 1,750 feet per second. Its 11 ounce incendiary or high explosive shell had an effect on aircraft structures which was truly devastating: against fighters or medium bombers a single hit was almost invariably sufficient to cause their destruction; against a four-engined heavy bomber, three or four hits were usually enough. During 1943 the MK 108 went into action fitted to the Messerschmitt 109, which carried one, and the Messerschmitt 110 and Focke Wulf 190 each

---

*It must be stressed that this was an *average* figure; some bombers were shot down with less hits, some returned with more.

The armament installation of the Focke Wulf 190A-3. The weapons mounted on top of the fuselage were mechanically-synchronised 7.9-mm Rheinmetall Borsig MG 17 machine guns, belt fed with 1,000 rounds per gun; these weapons were cocked and fired electro-pneumatically. The weapons fitted in the wing roots were 20-mm Mauser MG 151/20 cannon, belt fed with 200 rounds per gun. The Mauser was cocked and fired electrically, and fired electrically detonated ammunition. The latter made possible an extremely neat and reliable system of gun synchronisation: motor-driven cams simply interrupted the electrical circuit to the cartridge when a propeller blade was in the path of the shell, and re-made it when the blade was clear. The outboard weapons were unsynchronised 20-mm Oerlikon MG FF cannon, fed from 60-round drum magazines; these weapons had electro-pneumatic cocking and electrical firing.

Above:
An Avro Manchester bomber, showing six hits by 20-mm Oerlikon rounds; an average of twenty such hits were required to bring down a heavy bomber. *Lewin*

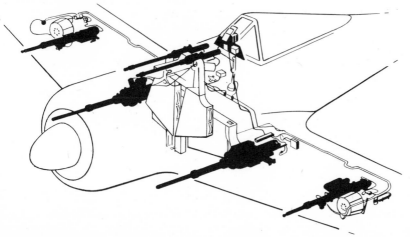

The Rheinmetall Borsig MK 108 cannon was the standard German bomber-destroying weapon during the final two years of the war; it fired 11 ounce high explosive or incendiary rounds at a rate of 660 per minute, with a muzzle velocity of 1,750 feet per second.

The effect of a single hit by an explosive round from an MK 108 on a Spitfire, fired during a ground trial carried out in Great Britain after the war; the tail has been severed almost completely. A single hit by such a round anywhere on the structure of a fighter or a medium bomber was usually sufficient to cause its destruction. Heavy bombers required an average of three hits with 30-mm ammunition to bring them down.

of which carried two. When the Me 262 jet fighter entered service in 1944 it carried the unprecedentedly heavy armament of four MK 108 guns; complete with the mountings and 360 rounds of ammunition, this battery weighed more than 1,100 pounds and could loose off a projectile weight of 96 pounds during a three-second burst. This was far and away the heaviest weight of fire possible for an operational gun-equipped fighter during the Second World War and when it struck home the effect on the victim was immediate, and usually catastrophic.

For all its destructive power, however, the MK 108 was not the complete answer to the Luftwaffe's problem. It was a low velocity weapon; to cover 1,000 yards its shells took over two and a half seconds, and they dropped nearly 100 feet before they got there. Clearly this was no weapon for long-range firing against moving targets, and to use it the German pilots still had to press home their attacks to well inside the range of the bombers' defensive fire.

In an attempt to knock the bombers out of formation at longer ranges, the Germans introduced a modified version of the 50-mm high velocity gun fitted to some of their tanks; with automatic loading and a new recoil system and barrel, this weapon became the BK 5 which was fitted into the Messerschmitt 410. The BK 5 fired shells weighing 3.5 pounds, large enough to knock down a heavy bomber with a single hit; leaving the muzzle with a velocity of 3,000 feet per second, they took just over a second to cover 1,000 yards and the gravity drop was only 24 feet. The rate of fire of only 45 rounds per minute – three in four seconds – was inordinately slow, but it was felt that the weapon's high velocity and destructive power would more than make up for this. The combination of the Me 410 and the BK 5 seemed to provide an ideal solution to the problem of stemming the American heavy bombers. But in war nothing stands still. By the time the new bomber destroyer was ready for action, in the spring of 1944, the American

A Messerschmitt 410 bomber destroyer, fitted with the BK 5 high velocity cannon which fired 50-mm shells weighing 3.5 pounds with a muzzle velocity of 3,000 feet per second but at a rate of only 45 per minute; a single hit by such a shell was likely to cause the destruction of even the largest aircraft. *via Redemann*

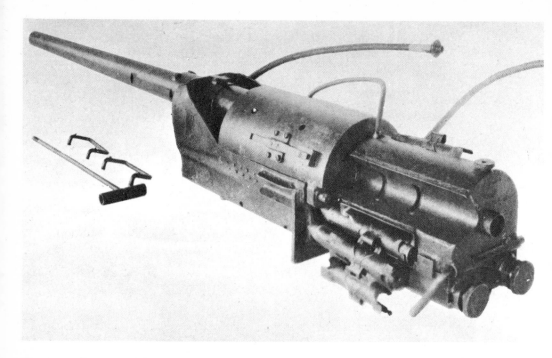

MG213 viewed from rear.

The outstanding Mauser MG 213 cannon, which fired 20-mm rounds with a muzzle velocity of 3,300 feet per second and at a rate of 1,200 per minute. The most advanced air-to-air cannon developed during the Second World War, it was just too late to see action.

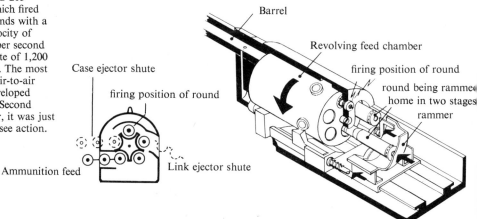

The revolving feed mechanism, which made possible the superb firing performance of the MG 213. In previous types of aircraft cannon the rounds were rammed into the breech and the empty cartridge was extracted after firing, in two movements of the breech block whose permissible reciprocal speed placed a physical limit to the maximum rate of fire that could be achieved. In the MG 213 the rotating cylinder, which formed both part of the feed mechanism and the breech, enabled five separate operations to take place simultaneously: while the round at 7 o'clock (viewed from the rear) was having its belt links removed, that at 5 o'clock was being partially rammed into the chamber, that at 2 o'clock was being fully rammed into the chamber, that at 12 o'clock was being fired and the empty cartridge case at 10 o'clock was being extracted.

The Japanese Ho 301 40-mm cannon, and the unusual cartridge-less round it fired; the propellant was housed in the rear of the projectile, and when it was fired the expanding gases impinged on the breech through the holes cut in the base. The Ho 301 had a rate of fire of 450 rounds per minute, remarkably high for a weapon of this calibre; but its muzzle velocity of only 760 feet per second restricted its effective engagement range to about 150 yards. *U.S.N.*

escort fighters were available over Germany in such numbers that slow deliberate attacks from behind the bomber formations were quite out of the question.

To replace the MK 108 as the standard German heavy cannon, the Mauser company came up with its *tour de force*, the magnificent MG 213. Initially produced with a calibre of 20 mm, the MG 213 was later to have been built in a 30-mm version as well. The 7.4 ounce shells of the 20-mm version were about twice as heavy as the normal projectile for this calibre, and the MG 213 spewed them out at a muzzle velocity of 3,300 feet per second and a rate of 1,200 per minute. The reason for this superb performance was that the weapon was fitted with a unique revolving chamber which served as both breech and part of the feed mechanism (see diagram). Just too late to see action during the Second World War, the MG 213 represented the zenith of aircraft gun design in 1945 and dominated it for more than a decade afterwards. After the war everybody copied its

Fighter Fire Power 1945. Projectile weight fired during a three-second burst; each 'shell' represents a projectile weight of two pounds.
1. Grumman F6F Hellcat (U.S.A.), six .5-inch (12.7 mm) machine guns, sixteen pounds. 2. Yak-3 (U.S.S.R.), one 20-mm cannon, two 12.7-mm machine guns, twenty pounds. 3. Focke Wulf 109D (Germany), two 20-mm cannon and two 13-mm machine guns, twenty-six pounds. 4. Mitsubishi J2M3 (Japan), four 20-mm cannon, thirty-one pounds. 5. Hawker Tempest V (Great Britain), four 20-mm cannon, forty pounds. 6. Messerschmitt 262 (Germany), four 30-mm cannon, ninety-six pounds.

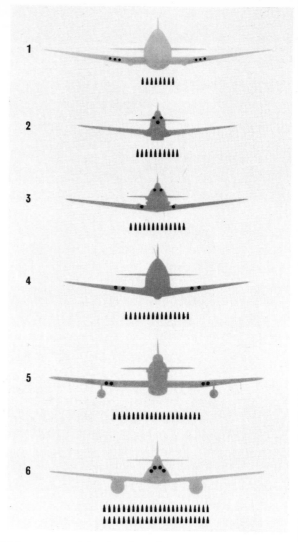

1 shell equals 2 pounds fired in 3 second burst

clever feed system, which was used in the American M-39, the British Aden, the French DEFA and the Russian NR 30 cannons.

In an effort to produce a really effective bomber destroyer, the Japanese fitted 30-mm, 37-mm and even 40-mm cannon to their fighters. The 30-mm Ho 105 was an effective weapon with a muzzle velocity somewhat higher than that of the German MK 108, though its rate of fire was lower. The 37-mm Ho 23 was greatly inferior, with a rate of fire of only 120 rounds per minute. The 40-mm Ho 301 fired an unusual type of round without a cartridge; the propellant was housed in a compartment at the rear of the projectile, and when it was fired the expanding gases impinged on the breech through holes cut in the rear of the round. This method had the advantage that there was no cartridge case to extract from the breech before the next round was rammed home; as a result the cannon had a rate

of fire of 450 rounds per minute, which was remarkably high for a weapon of this calibre. The great disadvantage was that the weapon had a muzzle velocity of only 760 feet per second, by far the lowest of any air-to-air gun used during the conflict, and because of this its effective range was limited to about 150 yards. During the war the Japanese heavy cannon saw only limited use, and they did not make any noticeable impression in combat before it ended.

A zero-deflection shot; when firing from almost exactly behind, no aim off was necessary. In this dramatic photograph the pilot is seen beating a hasty retreat from his battered Focke Wulf 190, following an attack by a Spitfire.

Sighting the Guns

The type of gunsight fitted to most fighters during the early 1930s was the so-called 'ring and bead', comprising a fixed metal foresight and rear sight positioned about three feet behind. To engage a target flying straight and level, from a fighter exactly behind or in front, simple sights like those fitted to infantry machine guns were quite adequate. But in air-to-air combat such an engagement was rare indeed; it was far more likely that the target would be moving with respect to its attacker, so if he was to hit it the fighter pilot had to aim at a point in front of his target removed by an amount known as the 'deflection angle'. To assist the pilot to judge his deflection angle one of his sighting heads, usually the rear one, was fitted with an outer ring whose size corresponded to the amount of aim off necessary to hit a target with a given crossing speed (typically 50 mph). It was a crude system, correct for only one crossing speed out of a wide range of possible ones, and to achieve accurate shooting it placed great demands on the ability and instinct of the pilot; indeed, the ability to calculate deflection angles accurately was to be one of the main points of difference between the ace fighter pilot and the also-ran, for air fighting up to almost the end of the Second World War. The ring and bead sight had other drawbacks: it could easily be knocked out of alignment; at the longer ranges the

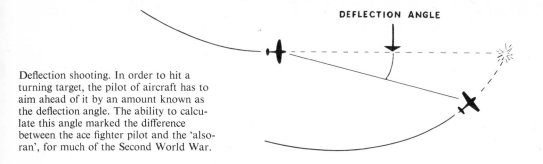

Deflection shooting. In order to hit a turning target, the pilot of aircraft has to aim ahead of it by an amount known as the deflection angle. The ability to calculate this angle marked the difference between the ace fighter pilot and the 'also-ran', for much of the Second World War.

metal sighting bead could obscure small targets completely; it was difficult for the pilot to focus on the rear sight close to his eye and simultaneously on the target which was, in optical terms, at infinity; and at night or under poor conditions of light it was sometimes difficult for the pilot to see his foresight, with the result that aimed fire was impossible.

During the 1930s the reflector sight became available, in which the deflection circle and the centre aiming point (together known as the 'sighting graticule') were produced by a small light projector and shone on to a reflector glass in front of the pilot; there was only one sighting point instead of two, but the system was arranged so that the pilot did not see the graticule unless his head was in the correct position behind the sight. The reflector sight was a great improvement over the ring and bead: its sighting head was stronger and far less likely to be knocked out of alignment; the pilot could adjust the brilliance of the light so that it did not obscure the target; its light graticule was focused at infinity, which was where the target was, and it was clearly visible at night or under poor conditions of light. By the outbreak of the Second World War all the major air forces had changed or were changing to the reflector sight: the British GM 2, the German Revi, the French Baille-Lemaire, the American ST 1A, the Italian San Giorgio or the Russian PBP-1. In several air forces the old ring and bead was retained as a back-up in case of a failure of the reflector sight, but the latter proved very reliable and as the war progressed the older system fell out of use.

The graticule of a reflector sight, showing the use of the ring to assist in calculating the deflection angle.

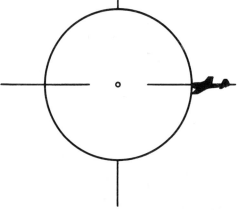

The cockpit of the
Focke Wulf 190A,
showing the glass of
the Revi reflector
sight protruding above
the cockpit coaming.

Although the reflector sight was an advance over the ring and bead, its substitution of a fixed circle of light for a fixed circle of metal did nothing to help the pilot with his most pressing problem: the accurate calculation of the deflection angle. Early in 1939 engineers and scientists at the Royal Aircraft Establishment at Farnborough began work on a completely new type of sight whose action depended on the fact that if a fighter pilot held his sight on a turning enemy, the rate of turn of his fighter was proportional to the deflection angle required to hit the target. A gyroscope was used to measure the rate of turn and it was arranged to tilt a mirror, which adjusted the position of the sight graticule on the reflector glass by the deflection angle thus found. The deflection angle varied with range, however, so the angle thus found was correct for only one value of range. To overcome this ranging problem the new sight had provision for the pilot to set on it the wing span of the enemy aircraft he was engaging; the diameter of the circular sighting graticule was made independent of the deflection angle, and instead depended on the size of the wing span of the enemy aircraft set on the sight. As he closed in on his enemy the fighter pilot, using a separate control mounted on his throttle, continually adjusted the size of the sighting graticule to keep it the same apparent diameter as the target's wing span. Since the wing span of the target was fixed and known and already set on the sight, the adjustment of the diameter of the graticule in this way 'told' the sight computer the exact range of the target; the sight computer then adjusted the amount of aim off to provide the correct deflection angle for this range.

It took three years of hard and often inspired work to perfect the new sight and get it into production; by the end of 1943 a version mass produced for fighters entered large-scale service in the Royal Air Force as the Gyro Gunsight Mark IID. Examples of the new sight were sent to the U.S.A., where they were produced in large numbers under the designations K-14 (U.S.A.A.F.) and Mark 18 (U.S.N.).

When it first appeared in service, the gyro gunsight was greeted with something less than enthusiasm. It was a bulky object and did not fit easily into the already-crowded fighter cockpits; moreover its location, immediately in front of the pilot's head, meant that it was likely to cause him severe facial injuries in the event of a crash landing. To use the gyro gunsight the fighter pilot had to follow his target in the turn for a minimum of one second, to give the sight time to calculate the deflection angle; this was in contrast to the older fixed-graticule sight, whose reading was instantaneous.

Once the average fighter pilot had mastered the use of the gyro gunsight, however, the accuracy of his shooting increased greatly. In 1944 an analysis of 130 combats by Mark IX Spitfires fitted with fixed-graticule sights revealed that there had been 34 kills, or 26 per cent of the total. Over a similar period one squadron equipped with the same type of aircraft fitted with the gyro gunsight was involved in 38 combats in which there were 19 kills, or 50 per cent of the total; the new sight had nearly doubled the effectiveness of air-to-air gunnery, making possible hits on evading targets at ranges as great as 600 yards and at deflection angles of over 50 degrees. There is the story of the U.S. VIIIth Air Force fighter unit where a replacement Mustang arrived fitted with the K-14; the commander, who regarded

The gyro gunsight brought about the greatest advance in sighting accuracy since the beginning of aerial gunnery. The pilot had only to set on the sight the wing span of his target, follow his enemy in the turn, and rotate the control mounted on his throttle lever until the circle of diamonds appeared to be the same size as the target's wing span; the computing mechanism in the sight then worked out the amount of 'lead' necessary for the bullets to strike the target. With the gyro gunsight the average squadron pilot was able to obtain hits at deflection angles that with fixed graticule sights had previously been possible only for the aces. *I.W.M.*

the gyro gunsight as 'just another gimmick', gave the aircraft to the unit's most junior pilot who used it on his first operational mission. During the combat that followed the new pilot surprised everyone, including himself, by shooting down a Fw 190 at a considerable angle of deflection. The following day, so the story goes, the new sight was airborne in the commander's own Mustang!

To the end of the war many of the Allied aces who had mastered the art of deflection shooting preferred to hang on to their old fixed-graticule sights; they saw little point in having to track their targets and wait for a gyro sight to produce an answer they knew instinctively. But the necessary mental gymnastics were beyond the average squadron pilot; to him the gyro gunsight was a great boon and with a little practice he was able to achieve the sort of results that previously had been possible only for those of exceptional ability.

Only the British and American air forces and their close allies made large-scale operational use of the gyro gunsight during the Second World War. Working independently the Askania company in Germany produced a sight using generally the same principles, designated the EZ 42 *Adler* (Eagle); at the end of the conflict the EZ 42 was only at the operational trials stage, however, and it still required a great deal of development work to make it work properly.

It would be difficult to exaggerate the importance of the gyro gunsight to the maintenance of Allied air supremacy during the closing stages of the war. Certainly the new-found increase in the accuracy of air-to-air gunnery went a long way towards compensating for the great difference in performance between the new German jet fighters and the Allied piston-engined types; as a result, during aerial combat, Allied fighters destroyed more than two German jet fighters for each Allied fighter or bomber the jet fighters were able to bring down.

Air-to-Air Bombs and Rockets

Before the war the use of air-to-air bombing as a means of splitting up bomber formations had been widely discussed in theoretical terms. The rewards from the successful use of these tactics promised to be great: the burst from a heavy anti-aircraft shell was lethal out to about 20 yards from the point of detonation; that from a 500 pound bomb was lethal out to about 100 yards. The difficulty, however, was to get this powerful explosion to happen close enough to the bombers to achieve any useful result. Quite apart from the problem of getting the bomb to pass close to a fast-moving target like a formation of aircraft, unless it scored a direct hit there was the problem of setting it off at precisely the right time; unlike the normal bomb which went off on hitting the ground, the air-to-air weapon had to explode during the split second during which the target was within range, or be wasted.

The Japanese were the prime exponents of air-to-air bombing during the Second World War, and went so far as to develop a series of weapons specially for this purpose. The first of these was the Type 99 No 3 Mark 3,

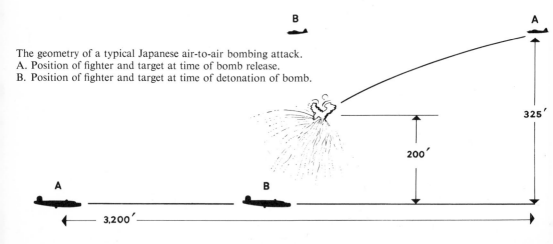

The geometry of a typical Japanese air-to-air bombing attack.
A. Position of fighter and target at time of bomb release.
B. Position of fighter and target at time of detonation of bomb.

which entered service in 1939 and weighed 83 pounds. It was shaped like a normal bomb except that it had offset tail fins to rotate it after release, and thus arm the clockwork tail fuse. When the bomb detonated, explosive charges at the centre and rear of the weapon blew outwards and forwards the 144 phosphorus incendiary pellets carried inside the casing. The bomb was effective out to about 75 yards beneath the point of detonation. A heavier weapon along the same lines was the Type 2 No 3 Mark 1, which weighed 551 pounds and was introduced in 1942; it carried 759 incendiary pellets, and was effective to about 200 yards beneath the point of detonation. Finally, at the end of the war, tests were in progress with the Type 5 No 25 Mark 29 bomb which weighed 551 pounds and contained 102 pounds of phosphorus incendiary material and 1,100 pellets. This bomb could be released in the normal way or, if the pilot was one of the Banzai breed, he could plunge into the enemy formation and at the flick of a switch blow up his aircraft, himself and, hopefully, one or two of the enemy.

Compared with the sustained efforts of the Japanese, the German attempts at air-to-air bombing amounted to nothing more than a few hastily conceived improvisations. During 1943 the Luftwaffe conducted operational trials using bombs ranging from anti-personnel weapons weighing a few pounds to 1,000 pounders. When air-to-air bombing was successful the effect, especially when the heavier bombs were used, was usually spectacular. But neither the German nor the Japanese air-to-air bombing was able to cause the destruction of many bombers, due to the aiming and detonation problems already mentioned. A simple proximity fuse would have made this type of attack much more effective, but neither power was able to perfect such a device before the end of the war.

Like air-to-air bombing, air-to-air rocketry had been widely discussed during the 1930s. The flatter trajectory of the rocket promised more accurate

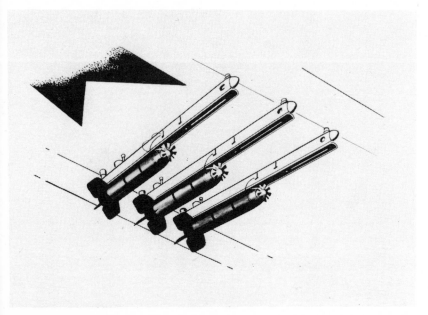

The Russian RS-82 rocket was the first such weapon to be used in the air-to-air role during the Second World War.

Missed! The distinctive octopus-like shape of an exploding Japanese air-to-air bomb, aimed at B-24 Liberators flying near the island of Truk in the Pacific. The 'tentacles' marked the paths of the burning phosphorus incendiary pellets. *U.S.A.A.F.*

Close-up of the
German 21-cm Wgr 21
rocket in its launching
tube under the wing
of a Focke Wulf 190.
These spin-stabilised
missiles were time-
fused, and the
difficulty of judging
accurately the range
of the target prevented
them from achieving
any great success
against the American
bomber formations.
via Schliephake

aiming, and if a direct hit could be achieved this would solve the problem of getting a timely detonation. The Russians were the first to use air-to-air rockets during the Second World War. Their RS-82 was $3\frac{1}{4}$ inches in diameter, $24\frac{1}{2}$ inches long and weighed 15 pounds of which just under a pound was explosive in the warhead; this was sufficient for a single hit to have a good chance of destroying a bomber target. The missile was fused to explode on impact, and six were carried on underwing racks on the Polikarpov I-16 and other Soviet fighters. Although some rather sweeping claims have been made for the success of this weapon in the air-to-air role, its all-burnt speed of 1,150 feet per second was not really high enough to give the flat trajectory required for this work; moreover a salvo of six was not sufficient to give a very high chance of a hit with the large dispersion errors that almost certainly existed. Probably the most reliable indicator of the effectiveness or otherwise of the RS-82 was that it was rarely if ever used in the air-to-air role during the latter half of the war.

The German introduction to air-to-air rocketry during the Second World War, like their introduction to air-to-air bombing, began with a hasty improvisation. Purpose-built air-to-air rockets take a long time to develop, so when in 1943 the Luftwaffe found that it had an urgent

requirement for its fighters to be able to hurl large amounts of explosive at the heavy bomber formations, from beyond the range of their defensive fire, it had to turn to the German army. The latter employed several types of rocket mortar of which one, the 21-cm Nebelwerfer 42, was suitable for modification for the air-to-air role. In the Luftwaffe the weapon was known as the Wgr 21; the spin-stabilised missile weighed 248 pounds at launch, of which 90 pounds comprised the warhead. A time fuse detonated the warhead at a preset distance between 600 and 1,200 yards from the point of launch, resulting in a lethal zone out to about 30 yards from the point of detonation. The single-engined Messerschmitt 109 and Focke Wulf 190 fighters could carry a single Wgr 21 in its tube launcher under each wing; the larger twin-engined Messerschmitt 110 and 410 types carried a pair of Wgr 21s under each wing. In combat, the performance of the Wgr 21 was disappointing. Its all-burnt speed of 1,020 feet per second was even lower than that of the Russian RS-82, and too low for accurate aiming. Moreover, as in the case of the air-to-air bombs, it proved extremely difficult for the pilot of the launching aircraft to judge the range so that they detonated in the right place; the majority of these missiles exploded harmlessly either short of the bombers or past them. As in the case of the air-to-air bombing

The Messerschmitt 110G, fitted with extra armament for the bomber-destroyer role, was the most heavily armed fighter in the world when it became operational in mid-1943. The example depicted carried a normal built-in armament of two 20-mm and two 30-mm cannon, in addition to which were a further two 20-mm cannon in the under-fuselage weapon tray and four 21 cm rockets under the wings. *Bundesarchiv*

The only air-to-air
rocket to enter service
during the Second
World War with a
velocity high enough
for accurate aiming
was the German R4M
Orkan (Tornado);
twelve of these folding-
fin missiles are
depicted on their
wooden launching
rack under the
starboard wing of an
Me 262 jet fighter. *via
Schliephake*

attacks, the rare successes with the Wgr 21 rockets were usually spectacular: during one of the early attacks with these weapons, on July 28th 1943, the missile exploded almost directly underneath one B-17 causing it to swing into one and then a second of the bombers in the formation and resulting in the destruction of all three.

The only purpose-built air-to-air rocket to enter service in the Luftwaffe was the R4M *Orkan* (Tornado), which was used during the closing months of the war. It was $2\frac{1}{8}$ inches in diameter and just under two feet eight inches long, and weighed a little over $7\frac{1}{2}$ pounds. With an all-burnt velocity of 1,740 feet per second, the R4M was considerably more accurate than either of the other two rockets we have examined. Moreover, because it weighed so little, it could be carried in large numbers by fighters; the Me 262 jet fighter carried twelve of these missiles under each wing, on wooden racks. The usual method of attack with these weapons was to ripple fire the entire complement of R4M at the bomber selected as target, from a range of 600 yards; after launch the rockets diverged slightly, to produce a circular pattern with a diameter roughly equivalent to the size of a four-engined bomber at that distance. The R4M warhead was impact fused, and the explosive content weighed about a pound; this was sufficient for a single hit to give a high probability of a kill against a heavy bomber.

During its short operational career the R4M proved highly successful. It did not, however, enable the German fighters to engage the American heavy bombers outside the range of their defensive fire. To fulfil this requirement the Rheinmetall Borsig company developed the R 100 BS, a large rocket weighing 242 pounds with a diameter of $8\frac{1}{4}$ inches and a length of just over 6 feet; the missile had an all-burnt velocity of 1,460 feet per second and a maximum effective range of about 2,000 yards. To overcome the knotty problem of accurate ranging, which had bedevilled the operations with the Wgr 21, the rather clever *Oberon* automatic firing system was produced for use with the R 100 BS.

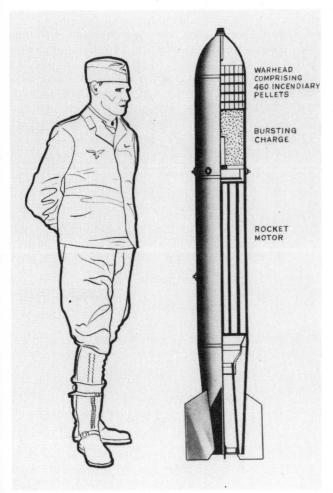

WARHEAD
COMPRISING
460 INCENDIARY
PELLETS

BURSTING
CHARGE

ROCKET
MOTOR

The German R 100BS incendiary shrapnel rocket, with its *Oberon* automatic firing system, could have caused serious damage to the American daylight bomber formations until suitable electronic countermeasures could be evolved.

The basis of *Oberon* was a simple radar set in the launching aircraft, with a fixed beam pointing forwards. Prior to the attack the pilot set the missile 'running time' on both its time fuse and the sighting computer. Once he had done this and armed the system, the pilot had only to hold the target in his gunsight. The radar continuously measured the range of the target, and the computer worked out the closing speed. When the fighter reached the firing range worked out by the computer, a pair of electrical contacts closed and the R 100 BS was launched automatically. The launching position was computed so that the missile, after having run for the previously-set time, was in a position about 85 yards short of the target when the time fuse detonated the warhead. The warhead comprised 460 incendiary pellets, which were blasted out in a cone-shaped pattern in front of the missile by a bursting charge; the pellets were designed to slice through the walls of the fuel tanks of the target aircraft and ignite the petrol.

The combination of *Oberon* and the R 100 BS constituted an effective and workable weapons system which was well within the state of the art in 1945. At the close of the war it was in full production, and it was intended that the Me 262 should carry five and the Me 410 six of these powerful rockets. There can be little doubt that had the Germans been able to get this weapons system into large-scale service it would, initially, have given the American daylight bomber crews a lot to worry about. But like almost any system employing radar, *Oberon* was vulnerable to countermeasures. Against attacks from the rear, bundles of 'Window' metal foil dropped from the bombers would probably have caused premature firing of the missiles; to counter head-on or rear attacks, a jamming transmitter would have been effective in neutralising the ranging system.

2 How they Compared.

*However absorbed a commander may be
in the elaboration of his own thoughts,
it is sometimes necessary
to take the enemy into account.*
WINSTON CHURCHILL

In this chapter the reader is able to see how versions of four of the most famous fighters of the Second World War, the German Focke Wulf 190A-3, the American P-51B Mustang, the British Tempest V and the Japanese A6M5 ('Zeke' 52) compared with the adversaries they met in combat and, in some cases, with their rivals in friendly air forces. The details are taken from recently released reports on comparative trials flown in Great Britain and the U.S.A. during the Second World War. Interesting though these trials undoubtedly are for the historian, it must be stressed that they were not written with him in mind; they constituted the basic Intelligence material vital for any fighter pilot who was to survive in action against an enemy bent on his destruction. And from the fighting man's point of view, a fairly good report immediately was worth far more than a magnificent report six months later.

In the nature of things, it was usually some time after their introduction into service that enemy fighters were captured in a state fit for flight trials. Thus there was a tendency for the comparative trials reports to present an optimistic picture from the point of view of the nation conducting them, since the latest equipment on one side was usually being compared with somewhat older equipment belonging to the other. For this reason the exact variant of each type involved in the trial is specified in the introduction; this is important because, taking the example of the Spitfire in its Mark V, Mark IX and Mark XIV versions *vis-à-vis* the Focke Wulf 190A-3, the former moved from inferiority, through parity, to definite superiority in a little over two years (in the meantime the Fw 190 had, of course, also improved). When considering the trials results, it was important to be sure exactly what was being compared with what.

The above limitations accepted, however, the trials reports still provide the most objective comparative assessment of the quality of the aircraft described. Combat reports could provide part of the picture but only a part, because they were liable to distortions of their own: unrelated factors such as the quality and training of the pilots, the numbers involved on each side and the rapidly moving tactical situation, all could combine to give an impression of the fighter types that was greatly removed from the truth.

The Focke Wulf 190A-3

The Focke Wulf 190A came as a nasty shock to the Royal Air Force when it was first used in action during the latter half of 1941. The example depicted is the A-5 sub-type, which featured water-methanol power boosting and was slightly faster than the A-3 used in the comparative trial.
Bundesarchiv

The Focke Wulf 190A-3 had an operational take-off weight of 8,770 pounds, which gave it a wing loading of just over 44 pounds per square foot. It was powered by a BMW 801D fourteen cylinder two-row radial engine with two-speed supercharging, which developed 1,700 horse-power for take-off and 1,440 horse-power at its rated altitude of 18,700 feet. The aircraft carried an armament of two 7.9-mm MG 17 machine guns fitted above the engine and synchronised to fire through the propeller arc, two 20-mm MG 151/20 cannon in the wing root also synchronised to fire through the propeller arc, and two 20-mm MG FF cannon in the wings outboard of the propeller arc. For his protection the pilot had a seat made of 8 mm thick armour plate, behind his head and shoulders was a shaped armour plate 13 mm thick, and the centre panel of his windscreen was of toughened glass 45 mm thick. Both fuel tanks, situated underneath the pilot's seat, were self sealing. The oil tank, situated in front of the engine just to the rear of the lip of the cowling, was protected by a ring of armour plate of varying thickness.

Layout of Focke Wulf 190 A3.

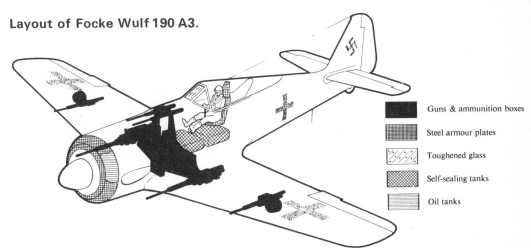

Guns & ammunition boxes

Steel armour plates

Toughened glass

Self-sealing tanks

Oil tanks

Deliveries of the Fw 190A-3 began in the spring of 1942, and the example used in the trial was captured in June after an inadvertent landing in England. The trial report was issued in August 1942. By that time, however, the A-3 version of the Fw 190 was on the point of being replaced on the production lines by the A-4 which featured water-methanol injection; this gave increases in speed of the order of 20 mph at altitudes up to the rated altitude of the engine.

Fw 190 versus Spitfire VB

The Fw 190 was compared with a Spitfire VB from an operational squadron for speed and all-round manoeuvrability at heights up to 25,000 feet. The Fw 190 is superior in speed at all heights, and the approximate differences are as follows:

At 1,000 ft the Fw 190 is 25–30 mph faster than the Spitfire VB
At 3,000 ft the Fw 190 is 30–35 mph faster than the Spitfire VB
At 5,000 ft the Fw 190 is 25 mph faster than the Spitfire VB
At 9,000 ft the Fw 190 is 25–30 mph faster than the Spitfire VB
At 15,000 ft the Fw 190 is 20 mph faster than the Spitfire VB
At 18,000 ft the Fw 190 is 20 mph faster than the Spitfire VB
At 21,000 ft the Fw 190 is 25 mph faster than the Spitfire VB
At 25,000 ft the Fw 190 is 20–25 mph faster than the Spitfire VB

Climb. The climb of the Fw 190 is superior to that of the Spitfire VB at all heights. The best speeds for climbing are approximately the same, but the angle of the FW 190 is considerably steeper. Under maximum continuous climbing conditions the climb of the Fw 190 is about 450 ft/min better up to 25,000 ft.

With both aircraft flying at high cruising speed and then pulling up into a climb, the superior climb of the Fw 190 is even more marked. When both aircraft are pulled up into a climb from a dive, the Fw 190 draws away very rapidly and the pilot of the Spitfire has no hope of catching it.

Dive. Comparative dives between the two aircraft have shown that the Fw 190 can leave the Spitfire with ease, particularly during the initial stages.

Manoeuvrability. The manoeuvrability of the Fw 190 is better than that of the Spitfire VB except in turning circles, when the Spitfire can quite easily out-turn it. The Fw 190 has better acceleration under all conditions of flight and this must obviously be most useful during combat.

When the Fw 190 was in a turn and was attacked by the Spitfire, the superior rate of roll enabled it to flick into a diving turn in the opposite direction. The pilot of the Spitfire found great difficulty in following this manoeuvre and even when prepared for it was seldom able to allow the correct deflection. A dive from this manoeuvre enabled the Fw 190 to draw away from the Spitfire which was then forced to break off the attack.

Several flights were carried out to ascertain the best evasive manoeuvres to adopt if 'bounced'. It was found that if the Spitfire was cruising at low speed and was 'bounced' by the Fw 190, it was easily caught up even if the Fw 190 was sighted when well out of range, and the Spitfire was then forced to take avoiding action by using its superiority in turning circles. If on the other hand the Spitfire was flying at maximum continuous cruising and was 'bounced' under the same conditions, it had a reasonable chance of avoiding being caught by opening the throttle and going into a *shallow* dive, provided the Fw 190 was seen in time. This forced the Fw 190 into a stern chase and although it eventually caught the Spitfire, it took some time and as a result was drawn a considerable distance away from its base. This is a particularly useful method of evasion for the Spitfire if it is 'bounced' when returning from a sweep. This manoeuvre has been carried out during recent operations and has been successful on several occasions.

If the Spitfire VB is 'bounced' it is thought unwise to evade by diving steeply, as the Fw 190 will have little difficulty in catching up owing to its superiority in the dive.

The above trials have shown that the Spitfire VB must cruise at high speed when in an area where enemy fighters can be expected. It will then, in addition to lessening the chances of being successfully 'bounced', have a better chance of catching the Fw 190, particularly if it has the advantage of surprise.

Fw 190 versus Spitfire IX

The Focke Wulf 190 was compared with a fully operational Spitfire IX for speed and manoeuvrability at heights up to 25,000 feet. The Spitfire IX at most heights is slightly superior in speed to the Fw 190 and the approximate differences in speeds at various heights are as follows:

At 2,000 ft the Fw 190 is 7–8 mph faster than the Spitfire IX
At 5,000 ft the Fw 190 and the Spitfire IX are approximately the same
At 8,000 ft the Spitfire IX is 8 mph faster than the Fw 190
At 15,000 ft the Spitfire IX is 5 mph faster than the Fw 190
At 18,000 ft the Fw 190 is 3 mph faster than the Spitfire IX
At 21,000 ft the Fw 190 and the Spitfire IX are approximately the same.
At 25,000 ft the Spitfire IX is 5–7 mph faster than the Fw 190

The Spitfire VB which, as the comparative trial showed, was quite outclassed by the Focke Wulf 190. The later Mark IX, fitted with the Merlin 61 engine with two-stage supercharging, had a performance closely comparable with that of the German fighter. *C. Brown*

Climb. During comparative climbs at various heights up to 23,000 feet, with both aircraft flying under maximum continuous climbing conditions, little difference was found between the two aircraft although on the whole the Spitfire IX was slightly better. Above 22,000 feet the climb of the Fw 190 is falling off rapidly, whereas the climb of the Spitfire IX is increasing. When both aircraft were flying at high cruising speed and were pulled up into a climb from level flight, the Fw 190 had a slight advantage in the initial stages of the climb due to its better acceleration. This superiority was slightly increased when both aircraft were pulled up into the climb from a dive.

It must be appreciated that the differences between the two aircraft are only slight and that in actual combat the advantage in climb will be with the aircraft that has the initiative.

Dive. The Fw 190 is faster than the Spitfire IX in a dive, particularly during the initial stage. This superiority is not as marked as with the Spitfire VB.

Manoeuvrability. The Fw 190 is more manoeuvrable than the Spitfire IX except in turning circles, when it is out-turned without difficulty.

The superior rate of roll of the Fw 190 enabled it to avoid the Spitfire IX if attacked when in a turn by flicking over into a diving turn in the opposite direction, and as with the Spitfire VB, the Spitfire IX had great difficulty in following this manoeuvre. It would have been easier for the Spitfire IX to follow the Fw 190 in a diving turn if its engine had been fitted with a negative 'G' carburettor, as this type of engine with the ordinary carburettor cuts very easily.

The Spitfire IX's worst heights for fighting the Fw 190 were between 18,000 and 22,000 feet and below 3,000 feet. At these heights the Fw 190 is a little faster.

Both aircraft 'bounced' one another in order to ascertain the best evasive tactics to adopt. The Spitfire IX could not be caught when 'bounced' if it was cruising at high speed and saw the Fw 190 when well out of range. When the Spitfire IX was cruising at low speed its inferiority in acceleration gave the Fw 190 a reasonable chance of catching it up and the same applied if the position was reversed and the Fw 190 was 'bounced' by the Spitfire IX, except that overtaking took a little longer.

The initial acceleration of the Fw 190 is better than the Spitfire IX under all conditions of flight, except in level flight at such altitudes where the Spitfire has a speed advantage and then, provided the Spitfire is cruising at high speed, there is little to choose between the acceleration of the two aircraft.

The general impression gained by the pilots taking part in the trials is that the Spitfire IX compares favourably with the Fw 190 and that provided the Spitfire has the initiative, it has undoubtedly a good chance of shooting the Fw 190 down.

Fw 190 versus Mustang IA (P-51A)

The Fw 190 was compared with a fully operational Mustang IA for speed and all-round performance up to 23,000 feet. There was little to choose between the aircraft in speed at all heights except between 10,000 and 15,000 feet, where the Mustang was appreciably faster. Approximate differences were as follows:

At 2,000 ft the Fw 190 is 2 mph faster than the Mustang IA
At 5,000 ft the Mustang is 5 mph faster than the Fw 190
At 10,000 ft the Mustang is 15 mph faster than the Fw 190
At 15,000 ft the Mustang is 10 mph faster than the Fw 190
At 20,000 ft the Fw 190 is 5 mph faster than the Mustang IA
At 23,000 ft the Fw 190 is 5 mph faster than the Mustang IA

Climb. The climb of the Fw 190 is superior to that of the Mustang IA at all heights. The best climbing speed for the Mustang is approximately 10 mph slower than that for the Fw 190; the angle is not nearly so steep and the rate of

climb is considerably inferior. When both aircraft are pulled up into a climb after a fast dive, the inferiority in the initial stage of the climb is not so marked, but if the climb is continued the Fw 190 draws away rapidly.

Dive. Comparative dives have shown that there is little to choose between the two aircraft and if anything the Mustang is slightly faster in a prolonged dive.

Manoeuvrability. The manoeuvrability of the Fw 190 is better than that of the Mustang except in turning circles where the Mustang is superior. In the rolling plane at high speed the Mustang compares more favourably with the Fw 190 than does the Spitfire.

The acceleration of the Fw 190 under all conditions of flight is slightly better than that of the Mustang and this becomes more marked when both aircraft are cruising at low speed.

When the Fw 190 was attacked by the Mustang in a turn, the usual manoeuvre of flicking into a diving turn in the opposite direction was not so effective against the Mustang as against the Spitfire, particularly if the aircraft were flying at high speed. The fact that the engine of the Mustang does not cut during the application of negative 'G' proved a great asset and gave the Mustang a reasonable chance of following the Fw 190 and shooting it down. It must be appreciated, however, that much depends on which aircraft has the initiative and that obviously the Fw 190 can escape if the Mustang is seen well out of range. The Fw 190 in this case will almost certainly utilise its superior climb.

Trials were carried out to ascertain the best manoeuvre to adopt when 'bounced'. If the Mustang was cruising at a high speed and saw the Fw 190

Although the Allison-engined 'A' version of the P-51 Mustang was not so potent as the later Merlin-engined version it was, as the comparative trial showed, a worthy opponent for the Focke Wulf 190A-3. *C. Brown*

about 2,000 yards away, it usually managed to avoid by opening up to full throttle and diving away, and once speed had been built up it was almost impossible for the Fw 190 to catch it. When the Mustang was 'bounced' by the Fw 190 when flying slowly, it was unable to get away by diving and was forced to evade by means of a quick turn as the Fw 190 came into firing range.

When the Fw 190 was 'bounced' by the Mustang, it could evade by using its superiority in the rolling plane and then pull up violently from the resultant dive into a steep climb which left the Mustang behind. If the Mustang is not seen until it is fairly close, it will get the chance of a short burst before it is out-climbed.

Against the Fw 190 the worst heights for the Mustang IA were above 20,000 feet and below 3,000 feet where the Fw 190 was slightly superior in speed. The best height for the Mustang was found to be between 5,C00 and 15,000 feet.

Fw 190 versus Lockheed P-38F

The Fw 190 was compared with an operationally equipped Lockheed P-38F flown by an experienced U.S. Army Air Force pilot. The two aircraft were compared for speed and all-round manoeuvrability at heights up to 23,000 feet. The Fw 190 was superior in speed at all heights up to 22,000 feet where the two aircraft were approximately the same. The difference in speed decreases as the P-38F gains altitude, until at 23,000 feet it is slightly faster. The approximate differences in speeds are as follows:

At 2,000 ft the Fw 190 is 15 mph faster than the P-38F
At 8,000 ft the Fw 190 is 15 mph faster than the P-38F
At 15,000 ft the Fw 190 is 5–8 mph faster than the P-38F
At 23,000 ft the P-38F is 6–8 mph faster than the Fw 190

Climb. The climb of the P-38F is not as good as that of the Fw 190 up to about 15,000 feet. Above this height the climb of the P-38F improves rapidly until at 20,000 feet it becomes superior. The best climbing speed for the P-38F is about 20 mph less than that of the Fw 190 and the angle approximately the same. The initial rate of climb of the Fw 190 either from level flight or a dive is superior to that of the P-38F at all heights below 20,000 feet, and above this height the climb of the P-38F becomes increasingly better.

Dive. Comparative dives between the two aircraft proved the Fw 190 to be better, particularly in the initial stage. During prolonged dives the P-38F on occasion was catching up slightly with the Fw 190, but during actual combat it is unlikely that the P-38F would have time to catch up before having to break off the attack.

Manoeuvrability. The manoeuvrability of the Fw 190 is superior to that of the P-38F, particularly in the rolling plane. Although at high speed the Fw 190 is superior in turning circles, it can be out-turned if the P-38F reduces its speed to about 140 mph, at which speed it can carry out a very tight turn which the Fw 190 cannot follow.

The acceleration of the two aircraft was compared and the Fw 190 was found to be better in all respects.

When the Fw 190 'bounced' the P-38F and was seen when over 1,000 yards away, the pilot's best manoeuvre was to go into a diving turn and if it found the Fw 190 was catching it up, to pull up into a spiral climb, flying at its slowest possible speed. Although time did not permit trials to be carried out with the Fw 190 being 'bounced' by the P-38F, it is thought that the P-38F would stand a reasonable chance of shooting down the Fw 190 provided it had a slight height advantage and the element of surprise. If the pilot of the Fw 190 sees the P-38F when it is just out of range, a quick turn in one direction followed by a diving turn in the opposite direction will give the P-38F a most difficult target, and as the acceleration and speed of the Fw 190 in a dive builds up very rapidly, it is likely to be able to dive away out of range.

The North American P-51B Mustang

The P-51B Mustang had an operational take-off weight of 10,100 pounds, which gave it a wing loading of nearly 44 pounds per square foot. The P-51B in the trial was powered by a V-1650/3 engine, the Packard licence-built version of the Rolls-Royce Merlin 61, which with two-stage supercharging developed 1,400 horse-power for take-off, 1,530 at 15,750 feet and 1,300 horse-power at 26,500 feet; thus at its best altitude the P-51B had about 300 horse-power more than the P-51A mentioned on page 108. The armament comprised four .5-inch Browning guns fitted in the wings and firing outside the propeller arc. For his protection the pilot had two pieces of armour plate behind his seat: one, 8 mm thick, extended from just below the bottom of the seat to a point just level with his shoulders; the other, 11 mm thick, was attached to the top of the other plate and protected his head. Other protection was provided by a 6 mm thick plate fitted to the firewall immediately in front of the cockpit, and the 38 mm thick toughened glass windscreen. Immediately forward of the coolant tank at the front of the engine was a small segment of 6-mm thick armour plate. All internal fuel tanks were self sealing.

Deliveries of the P-51B began in the late autumn of 1943, and the trials report was issued in March 1944. By that time the Focke Wulf 190A-4 and A-8 versions with water-methanol power boosting were well established in service, which were faster than the A-3 in the trial by 20–30 mph up to 18,700 feet. The Messerschmitt 109G-2 in the trial was an early 1943 sub-type; by March 1944 later versions such as the G-6 and G-10 were in service fitted with water-methanol or nitrous oxide power boosting which in their basic versions gave top speeds very nearly as great as that of the P-51B. The trouble with both German fighters was that in their bomber-destroyer versions they were loaded down with heavy cannon, and it was this that reduced their performance and made them relatively easy meat for the unhindered Mustangs.

The layout of the P-51B Mustang.

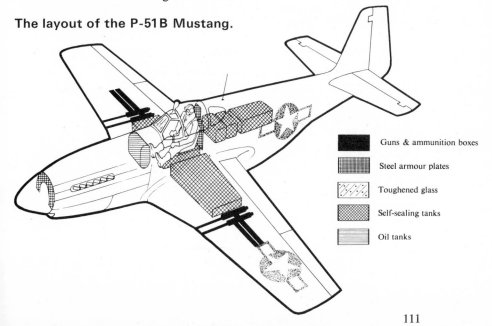

■	Guns & ammunition boxes
▦	Steel armour plates
▨	Toughened glass
▨	Self-sealing tanks
▤	Oil tanks

P-51B compared with Spitfire IX

The Merlin-engined P-51B Mustang whose superior fighting performance, coupled with superb range, enabled the Allies to establish air superiority over the German homeland during the late spring of 1944. The P-51B had a maximum speed of 440 mph at 30,000 feet. *via Holmes*

A very close comparison can be made because the two engines are of very similar design and capacity. The tactical differences are caused chiefly by the fact that the Mustang is a much cleaner aircraft, is slightly heavier, and has a higher wing loading than the Spitfire IX (43.8 lbs per sq ft of the Mustang, against 31 lbs per sq ft).

Endurance. The Mustang with maximum fuel load has between $1\frac{1}{2}$ and $1\frac{3}{4}$ the range of the Spitfire IX with maximum fuel load. The fuel and oil capacities are 154 Imp (183 U.S.) gallons and 11.2 Imp (13.3 U.S.) gallons respectively, as opposed to 85 Imp (101 U.S.) gallons and 7.5 Imp (9 U.S.) gallons of the Spitfire IX, both without long-range tanks. With long-range tanks, the Mustang can carry a total of 279 Imp (330 U.S.) gallons of petrol ($2 \times 62\frac{1}{2}$ Imp (75 U.S.) gallon long-range tanks) as opposed to the Spitfire IX's maximum of 177 Imp (210 U.S.) gallons (1×90 Imp (107 U.S.) gallon 'slipper' tank).

The fuel consumption at similar boost and rev settings is approximately the same for the two aircraft, but the Mustang is approximately 20 mph faster in level flight. Therefore, if the ranges are compared directly according to the fuel capacities of the two aircraft when the long-range tanks are fitted, the Mustang will still have something in hand.

Speeds. The official speed curves are not yet available. This Unit's speed runs have therefore not been confirmed. They show, however, that in general for the

same engine settings the Mustang is always 20–30 mph faster in level flight for all heights. This is also true for the maximum engine setting of 3,000 rpm 67″ (+18 lbs boost) or whatever is available, depending on the height. The best performance heights are similar, being between 10,000 and 15,000 ft, and between 25,000 and 32,000 ft.

Climbs. The Mustang has a considerably lower rate of climb at full power at all heights (in a formation take-off, the Spitfire IX maintains formation with 5 lbs less boost). At other engine settings and 175 mph, the two aircraft have a similar climb. The Mustang has, however, a better zoom climb in that it can dive 5,000 feet or more and regain its original altitude at a greater speed. It needs less increase of power to regain its previous altitude and speed.

Dives. The Mustang pulls away very rapidly in a slight dive. At the same revs the Spitfire IX requires from 4 to 6 lbs more boost to remain in formation.

Turning circle. The Mustang is always out-turned by the Spitfire IX. Use of flaps on the Mustang does not appear to improve the turning circle. There is adequate warning of the high speed stall in the form of elevator buffeting, followed by tail buffeting.

Rate of roll. Although the ailerons feel light, the Mustang cannot roll as quickly as the Spitfire IX at normal speeds. The ailerons stiffen up only slightly at high speeds and the rates of roll become the same at about 400 mph.

Although the P-51B was a potent enough fighter, there was still considerable development potential in this aircraft. The P-51H, which was ready for operations just in time for the final stages of the war in the Pacific, had a maximum speed of 487 mph at 25,000 feet, on the 2,218 horse power from a water-methanol boosted Packard V-1650-9 Merlin. This aircraft was armed with six .5-inch machine guns, and loaded weighed 9,500 pounds. *North American*

Fire-power. The fire-power of the Mustang consists of four .5 Brownings in the wings. This is very little compared with the Spitfire.

P-51B compared with Spitfire XIV

Maximum endurance. By comparison the Spitfire XIV has no endurance.
Maximum speed. There is practically nothing to choose in maximum speed.
Maximum climb. The Spitfire XIV is very much better.
Dive. As for the Spitfire IX. The Mustang pulls away, but less markedly.
Turning circle. The Spitfire XIV is the better.
Rate of roll. The advantage tends to be with the Spitfire XIV.
Conclusion. With the exception of endurance, no conclusions should be drawn, as these two aircraft should never be enemies. The choice is a matter of taste.

P-51B versus Fw 190

Maximum speed. The Fw 190 is nearly 50 mph *slower* at all heights, increasing to 70 mph above 28,000 feet. It is anticipated that the new Fw 190 (DB 603)* might be slightly faster below 27,000 feet but slower above that altitude.
Climb. There appears to be little to choose in the maximum rate of climb. It is anticipated that the Mustang will have a better maximum climb than the new Fw 190 (DB 603). The Mustang is considerably faster at all heights in a zoom climb.
Dive. The Mustang can always out-dive the Fw 190.

*This was a reference to the long-awaited in-line engine powered Fw 190, of which the Allied Intelligence services had obtained some information. The D version of the Fw 190 did not go into service until the late summer of 1944, and when it did it was powered by the Junkers Jumo 213.

Turning circle. Again, there is not much to choose. The Mustang is slightly better. When evading an enemy aircraft with a steep turn, a pilot will always out-turn the attacking aircraft initially because of the difference in speeds. It is therefore still a worth-while manoeuvre with the Mustang when attacked.

Rate of roll. Not even the Mustang approaches the Fw 190.

Conclusions. In the attack, a high speed should be maintained or regained in order to regain height initiative. A Fw 190 could not evade by diving alone. *In defence a steep turn followed by a full throttle dive should increase the range before regaining height and course.* Dog-fighting is not altogether recommended. Do not attempt to climb away without at least 250 mph showing initially. Unfortunately, there is not enough information on the new Fw 190 (DB 603) for any positive recommendations to be made.

P-51B versus Me 109G

Maximum speed. The Mustang is faster at all heights. Its best heights, by comparison, are below 16,000 ft (30 mph faster approx.) and above 25,000 ft (30 mph increasing to 50 mph at 30,000 ft).

Maximum climb. This is rather similar. The Mustang is very slightly better above 25,000 ft but inclined to be worse below 20,000 feet.

Zoom climb. Unfortunately the Me 109G appears to have a very good high speed climb, making the two aircraft similar in a zoom climb.

Dive. On the other hand in defence the Mustang can still increase the range in a prolonged dive.

Turning circle. The Mustang is greatly superior.

Rate of roll. Not much to choose. In defence (in a tight spot) a rapid change of direction will throw the Me 109G's sight off. This is because the 109G's maximum rate of roll is embarrassing (the wing slots keep opening).

With the provision of nitrous oxide or water-methanol injection the Messerschmitt 190G-6 (depicted), the main production version of this fighter during 1943, was somewhat faster in level flight than the G-2 flown in the comparative fighting trial against the P-51B. However, the weight of the extra armament demanded for the bomber-destroyer role reduced the climbing performance and manoeuvrability of the later model. This G-6 carried a built-in armament of one 30-mm cannon and two 13-mm machine guns, and carried an additional 20-mm cannon in the blister under each wing. *via Schliephake*

Conclusions. In attack, the Mustang can always catch the Me 109G, except in any sort of climb (unless there is a high overtaking speed). In defence, a steep turn should be the first manoeuvre, followed, if necessary, by a dive (below 20,000 feet). A high speed climb will unfortunately not increase the range. If above 25,000 ft keep above by climbing or all-out level.

Combat Performance with Long-Range Tanks

Speed. There is a serious loss of speed of 40–50 mph at all engine settings and heights. It is, however, still faster than the Fw 190 (BMW 801) above 25,000 ft although slower than the Me 109G.

Climb. The rate of climb is greatly reduced. It is outclimbed by the Fw 190 (BMW 801), Me 109G and the Fw 190 (DB 603). The Mustang is still good in a zoom climb (attack), but is still outstripped (defence), if being followed all the way by the Fw 190 (BMW 801) and definitely outstripped by the Me 109G.

Dive. So long as the tanks are fairly full, the Mustang still beats the Fw 190 (BMW 801) and the Me 109G in a power dive.

Turning circle. The tanks do not make quite so much difference as one might expect. The Mustang can at least turn as tightly as the Fw 190 (BMW 801) without stalling out and therefore definitely more tightly than the Me 109G.

Rate of roll. General handling and rate of roll are very little affected.

Conclusions. The performance of the Mustang is greatly reduced when carrying drop-tanks. Half-hearted attacks could still be evaded by a steep turn, but determined attacks would be difficult to avoid without losing height. It is still a good attacking aircraft especially if it has the advantage of height.

The Hawker Tempest V

The Hawker Tempest V had an operational take-off weight of 11,400 pounds, which gave it a wing loading of 37.7 pounds per square foot. It was powered by a Napier Sabre IIB twenty-four cylinder sleeve valve engine, which developed 2,400 horse-power at sea level and 2,045 horse-power at 13,750 feet. The Tempest was a thinner winged and generally improved development of the earlier Typhoon, which had not enjoyed great success as a fighter although it did well as a ground attack aircraft. Like the Typhoon the Tempest carried an armament of four 20-mm Hispano cannon; but those fitted to the latter were of the newer Mark V type, which had a rate of fire 15 per cent greater for a weight of one quarter less than was the case for the earlier Mark II. For his protection the pilot had 6-mm armour plating behind his back and 9-mm plating behind his head. Other pieces of armour were arranged throughout the aircraft to protect the ammunition boxes and other vulnerable areas. The pilot's windscreen was of toughened glass, and all the fuel tanks were self-sealing.

The Tempest V was employed mainly as a low and medium altitude fighter. It became operational in March 1944, and the trials report was issued at the end of that month. The versions of the Focke Wulf 190 and the Messerschmitt 109 employed in the trial were early ones, and the remarks made when they were compared with the P-51B (see page 111) apply in this case.

Opposite:

The Hawker Tempest V was the best British low altitude fighter to see large-scale service during the Second World War, with a maximum speed of 392 mph at sea level and 435 mph at 17,000 feet. *C. Brown*

The layout of the Tempest V.

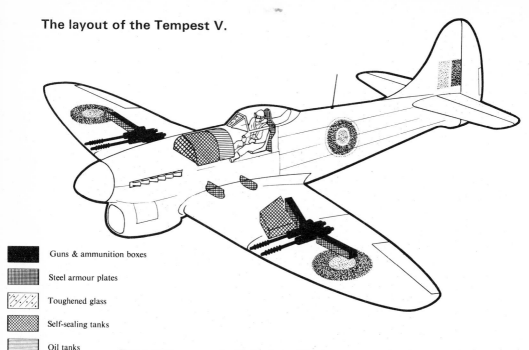

- ■ Guns & ammunition boxes
- ▤ Steel armour plates
- ▨ Toughened glass
- ▧ Self-sealing tanks
- ▤ Oil tanks

Tempest V compared with Typhoon IB

The comparison is fairly close and clear because the aircraft are fairly similar, differing chiefly in wing section only. The wing loadings are similar (37.7 pounds for the Tempest, and 39.7 pounds for the Typhoon).

Radius of action. The Tempest, as it stands (no nose tank or long-range tanks) has approximately the same range as the Typhoon IB without long-range tanks. The fuel and oil capacities of the Tempest are 132 Imp (157 U.S.) gallons and 14 Imp (16.7 U.S.) gallons respectively, compared with 154 Imp (184 U.S.) and 16 Imp (19 U.S.) gallons of the Typhoon. The fact that the Tempest cruises at 15–20 mph faster than the Typhoon at the same engine settings approximately cancels out the discrepancy in fuel load. A Tempest fitted with a nose tank (30 Imp gallons) and two 45 Imp (55 U.S.) gallon long-range tanks (252 Imp gallons total) would have about $1\frac{1}{4}$ times the range of the Typhoon IB with maximum fuel load (243 Imp gallons total).

Speeds. According to the official speed curves, the maximum speeds of the Tempest at all heights are 15–20 mph faster. This is also true for all intermediate settings.

Climbs. The Tempest climbs at a slightly steeper angle and at the same airspeed producing 200–300 ft increase in the maximum rate of climb. Because of its greater cleanliness, its zoom climb is much better.

Dive. For the same reasons as the zoom climb, the Tempest pulls ahead. As the speed is increased it does so more rapidly. In fact it has the best acceleration in the dive yet seen at this Unit.

Turning circle. Very similar. Any difference appears to be in favour of the Typhoon. This is too slight to alter the combat tactics.

Rate of roll. The Tempest has the better rate of roll at all speeds.

Conclusions. Taken all round, the Tempest V is a great improvement on the Typhoon IB.

Tempest V compared with P-51B Mustang

Range and endurance. By comparison the Tempest without nose tank or long-range tanks has no range. When this extra fuel is available it should have a range of little more than half that of the Mustang fitted with two 62½ Imp (75 U.S.) gallon long-range tanks, but without the extra 71 Imp (84 U.S.) gallon body tank.

Maximum speed. The Tempest V is 15–20 mph faster up to 15,000 feet, there is then no choice to 24,000 feet when the Mustang rapidly pulls ahead, being about 30 mph faster at 30,000 feet.

Climbs. These compare directly with the results of the speed tests. At similar performance height the Tempest has a better zoom climb.

Turning circle. The Tempest V is not quite as good as the Mustang.

Rate of roll. The Tempest is not so good.

Conclusions. The Mustang has a superior range of action and general performance about 24,000 ft. Conclusions should not be drawn below this height, but the Tempest has a much better rate of climb and speed below 10,000 feet.

Tempest V compared with Spitfire XIV

Range and endurance. Rough comparisons have been made at the maximum cruising conditions of both aircraft. It is interesting that the indicated airspeed of each is about 280 mph and the range of each is about identical; both with full fuel load (including long-range tanks) and without (also no nose-tank – Tempest).

Maximum speed. From 0–10,000 feet the Tempest V is 20 mph faster than the Spitfire XIV. There is then little to choose until 22,000 feet, when the Spitfire

A Tempest V (nearest the camera) in formation with an example of the earlier Typhoon, from which it was developed. Although the two fighters were powered by Sabre engines developing approximately the same power, the cleaner Tempest was about 20 mph faster. *I.W.M.*

119

XIV becomes 30–40 mph faster, the Tempest's operational ceiling being about 30,000 feet as opposed to the Spitfire XIV's 40,000 feet.

Maximum climb. The Tempest is not in the same class as the Spitfire XIV. The Tempest V, however, has a considerably better zoom climb, holding the higher speed throughout the manoeuvre. If the climb is prolonged until climbing speed is reached then, of course, the Spitfire XIV will begin to catch up and pull ahead.

Dive. The Tempest V gains on the Spitfire XIV.

Turning circle. The Spitfire XIV easily out-turns the Tempest.

Rate of roll. The Spitfire XIV rolls faster at speeds below 300 mph but definitely more slowly at speeds greater than 350 mph.

Conclusions. The tactical attributes of the two aircraft being completely different, they require separate handling technique in combat. For this reason, Typhoon squadrons should convert to Tempests, and Spitfire squadrons to Spitfire XIVs, and definitely never vice-versa, or each aircraft's particular advantages would not be appreciated. Regarding performance, if correctly handled, the Tempest is better below about 20,000 feet and the Spitfire XIV is better above that height.

Tempest V versus Fw 190

Maximum speed. The Tempest is nearly 50 mph faster at all heights. It is estimated that the Tempest V may be very slightly faster than the new Fw 190 (DB 603) up to 20,000 feet.

Climb. Except below 5,000 feet the Fw 190 (BMW 801) has a slightly better maximum rate of climb. Because of the Tempest V's speed and clean lines, however, the Tempest has a markedly better zoom climb, where the speed is kept high. Against the new Fw 190 (DB 603) it is estimated that the Tempest will have a markedly superior climb below 5,000 feet, but a similar maximum climb above that height.

Dive. The Tempest pulls away rapidly in a dive from all heights.

Turning circles. There is very little difference in turning circles between the two aircraft. If anything, a very slight advantage lies with the Tempest.

Rate of roll. The Tempest V cannot compare with the Fw 190.

Conclusions. Similar tactics should be used against the Fw 190 as used by the Typhoon squadrons, advantage being taken of high speed. Such handling should prove most effective. The Tempest has an exceptional ground height performance even (estimated) against the new Fw 190 (DB 603).

Tempest V versus Messerschmitt 109G

Maximum speed. The Tempest V is 40–50 mph faster up to 20,000 feet when the difference in speed rapidly diminishes.

Climb. The Tempest V is behind the Me 109G at all heights, but being almost similar below 5,000 feet. The Tempest is only slightly better in a zoom climb if the two aircraft start at the same speed, but if the Tempest has an initial advantage, it will hold this advantage easily providing the speed is kept over 250 mph.

Dive. The initial acceleration of the Tempest is not marked, but a prolonged dive brings the Tempest well ahead.

Turning circle. The Tempest is slightly better, the Me 109G being embarrassed by its slots opening near the stall.

Rate of roll. At normal speeds there is nothing in it, but at speeds over 350 mph the Tempest could get away from the Me 109G by making a quick change of bank and direction.

Conclusions. In the attack, the Tempest can always follow the Me 109 except in a slow, steep climb. In the combat area the Tempest should maintain a high speed, and in defence may do anything except attempt to climb at slow speed.

Opposite:

A trio of Tempests of No 501 Squadron, Royal Air Force.
C. Brown

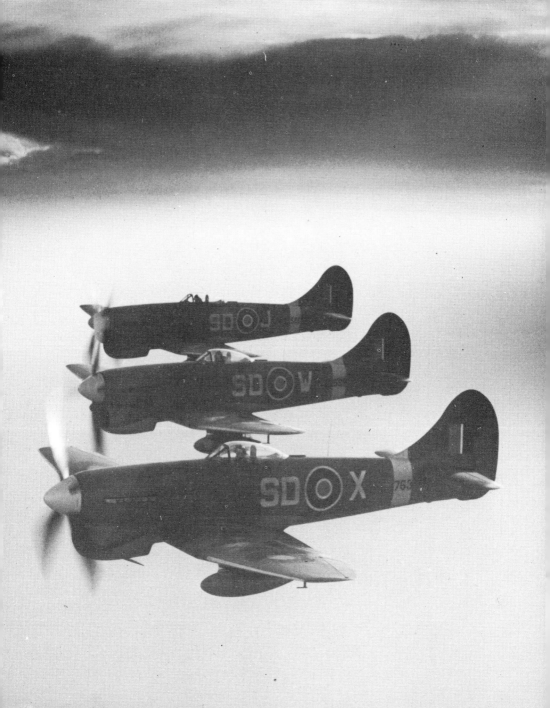

The Mitsubishi A6M5 (Allied Code Name Zeke 52)

The A6M5 was equipped to operate from aircraft carriers, and during the trials it was flown against similarly-equipped Allied fighters. It had an operational take-off weight of 6,094 pounds, which gave it a wing loading of just under 25 pounds per square foot (in each case these figures were far lower than those for comparable Allied or German fighters of the late war period). The A6M5 was powered by a Nakajima Sakae 31-A fourteen cylinder two-row radial engine with a two-speed supercharger, which developed 1,130 horse-power for take-off, 1,100 horse-power at 9,300 feet and 980 horse-power at 19,600 feet. It is interesting to note that the A6M5 of 1944 had wing and power loadings closely comparable with those of the Mark I Spitfire of 1939; the developed Seafire LIIC was, of course, somewhat heavier.

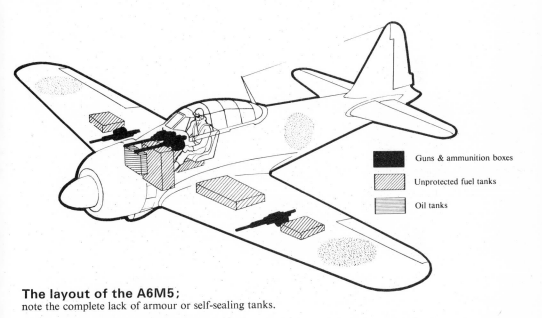

Guns & ammunition boxes

Unprotected fuel tanks

Oil tanks

The layout of the A6M5;
note the complete lack of armour or self-sealing tanks.

The armament carried by the A6M5 comprised two 7.7-mm Type 97 machine guns fitted on top of the engine and synchronised to fire through the airscrew arc, and two 20-mm Type 99 cannon in the wings outboard of the propeller arc. The aircraft carried no protective armour plate or toughened glass, and the fuel tanks were not self-sealing.

Deliveries of the A6M5 began in the spring of 1944 and the example used in the trial was captured during the invasion of Saipan in June 1944. The reports on the trials were issued in the autumn of 1944. By that time newer models of the A6M5 had appeared but, because they carried heavier armaments and in some cases limited armour protection, there was no major increase in performance over the version tested. In some fighter

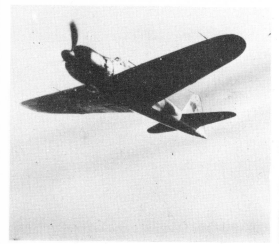

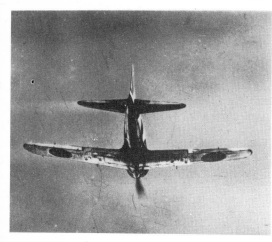

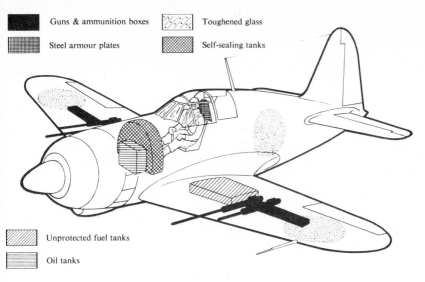

Guns & ammunition boxes

Toughened glass

Steel armour plates

Self-sealing tanks

Unprotected fuel tanks

Oil tanks

In the summer of 1944 the Mitsubishi J2M3 (Allied code-name 'Jack') began to replace the A6M5 and earlier types in Japanese Navy units. This fighter carried self-sealing tanks, and a little armour protection for the pilot. It was powered by a 1,820 horse-power Mitsubishi Kasei 23a engine, and had a maximum speed of 371 mph at 19,400 feet. Armed with four 20-mm cannon, the J2M3 had a loaded weight of 7,573 pounds.

units of the Imperial Japanese Navy, however, the early versions of the A6M5 were being replaced by higher performance types such as the Kawanishi N1K1 ('George') and the Mitsubishi J2M3 ('Jack').

Zeke 52 versus F4U-1D Corsair

Maximum speed. The F4U-1D was much faster than the Zeke 52 at all altitudes:
At sea level the F4U-1D was 48 mph faster than the Zeke 52
At 5,000 ft the F4U-1D was 42 mph faster than the Zeke 52
At 10,000 ft the F4U-1D was 58 mph faster than the Zeke 52
At 15,000 ft the F4U-1D was 70 mph faster than the Zeke 52
At 20,000 ft the F4U-1D was 78 mph faster than the Zeke 52
At 25,000 ft the F4U-1D was 80 mph faster than the Zeke 52
At 30,000 ft the F4U-1D was 74 mph faster than the Zeke 52
The top speeds obtained were 413 mph at 20,400 feet for the F4U-1D and 335 mph at 18,000 feet for the Zeke 52.
Climb. The best climb of the F4U-1D was equal to that of the Zeke 52 up to 10,000 feet, about 750 ft/min better at 18,000 feet, and about 500 ft/min better at 22,000 feet and above. The best climbing speeds of the F4U-1D and the Zeke 52 were found to be 158 and 123 mph indicated, respectively.
Dive. Initial dive accelerations of the Zeke 52 and the F4U-1D were about equal, after which the F4U-1D was far superior. The F4U-1D was slightly superior in zooms after dives.
Turning circle. The Zeke 52 was greatly superior to the F4U-1D in slow speed turns at low and medium altitudes, its advantage decreasing to only a slight margin at 30,000 feet. In slow speed turns it could gain one turn in three and one-half at 10,000 feet. At speeds around 205 mph, however, the F4U-1D could, by using flaps, stay with the Zeke 52 for about one-half turn, or until the speed fell to 175 mph.
Rate of roll. The rolls of the Zeke 52 were equal to those of the F4U-1D at speeds under 230 mph and inferior above that speed, due to the high control forces.
Manoeuvrability. The manoeuvrability of the Zeke 52 is remarkable at speeds below about 205 mph, being far superior to that of the F4U-1D. Its superiority, however, diminishes with increased speed, due to its high control forces, and the F4U-1D has the advantage at speeds above 230 mph.

Opposite:

The Mitsubishi A6M5 (Allied code-name 'Zeke 52'), developed from the famous Zero fighter, was in large-scale service in the Japanese Navy in the summer of 1944. It was, however, quite outclassed by the latest Allied shipborne fighters which confronted it.

The Chance Vought
F4U-1D Corsair was
powered by a 2,250
horse-power Pratt and
Whitney R 2800-8W
engine, and had a
maximum speed of
413 mph at 20,000
feet. It carried an
armament of six .5-
inch machine guns,
and loaded weighed
12,039 pounds. *L.T.V.*

Vision. The Zeke 52 was considered to permit better vision in all respects, the rear vision being good due to the use of a bubble canopy and the complete absence of armour behind the pilot's head. There was no rear vision mirror installed in the Zeke 52 tested. The small gunsight did not interfere with forward vision.

Conclusions. Do not dog-fight with the Zeke 52. Do not try to follow a loop or half-roll with pull-through. When attacking use your superior power and high speed performance to engage at the most favourable moment. To evade a Zeke 52 on your tail, roll and dive away into a high speed turn.

Zeke 52 versus F6F-5 Hellcat

Maximum speed. The F6F-5 was much faster than the Zeke 52 at all altitudes.

At sea level the F6F-5 was 41 mph faster than the Zeke 52
At 5,000 ft the F6F-5 was 25 mph faster than the Zeke 52
At 10,000 ft the F6F-5 was 45 mph faster than the Zeke 52
At 15,000 ft the F6F-5 was 62 mph faster than the Zeke 52
At 20,000 ft the F6F-5 was 69 mph faster than the Zeke 52
At 30,000 ft the F6F-5 was 66 mph faster than the Zeke 52

Top speeds attained were 409 mph at 21,600 feet for the F6F-5 and 335 mph at 18,000 ft for the Zeke 52.

Climb. The Zeke 52 climbed about 600 ft/min better than the F6F-5 up to 9,000 feet, after which the advantage fell off gradually until the two aircraft were about

equal at 14,000 feet, above which altitude the F6F-5 had the advantage, varying from 500 ft/min better at 22,000 feet to about 250 ft/min better at 30,000 feet. The best climbing speeds of the F6F-5 and the Zeke 52 were found to be 152 and 123 mph, respectively.

Dive. Initial dive accelerations of the Zeke 52 and the F6F-5 were about equal, after which the F6F-5 was far superior. The F6F-5 was slightly superior in zooms after dives.

Turning circle. The Zeke 52 was greatly superior to the F6F-5 in slow speed turns at low and medium altitudes, its advantage decreasing to about parity at 30,000 feet. In slow speed turns it could gain one turn in three and one-half at 10,000 feet.

Rate of roll. Rolls of the Zeke 52 were equal to those of the F6F-5 at speeds under 235 mph and inferior above that speed, due to the high control forces.

Manoeuvrability. The manoeuvrability of the Zeke 52 is remarkable at speeds below about 205 mph, being far superior to that of the F6F-5. Its superiority, however, diminishes with increased speed, due to its high control forces, and the F6F-5 has the advantage at speeds above 235 mph.

Vision. As for the F4U-1D.

Conclusions. Do not dog-fight with the Zeke 52. Do not try to follow a loop or half-roll with a pull-through. When attacking use your superior power and high speed performance to engage at the most favourable moment. To evade a Zeke 52 on your tail, roll and dive away into a high speed turn.

An F6F-5 Hellcat with an under-fuselage drop tank being prepared for catapulting from a U.S. Navy escort carrier; catapulting was often used to get heavily laden aircraft airborne, under light wind conditions, from the smaller types of aircraft carrier. Powered by a 2,000 horse-power Pratt and Whitney R-2800-10W engine, the F6F-5 had a maximum speed of 409 mph at 21,600 feet. It carried an armament of six .5-inch machine guns, and loaded weighed 12,500 pounds. *U.S.N.*

The FM-2 version of the famous Wildcat fighter was powered by a 1,350 horse-power Wright Cyclone engine, which gave it a maximum speed of 321 mph at 13,000 feet. Armed with four .5-inch machine guns, it had a loaded weight of 7,487 pounds. *I.W.M.*

Zeke 52 versus FM-2 Wildcat

Maximum speed. The Zeke 52 was progressively faster than the FM-2 above 5,000 feet.

At sea level the FM-2 was 6 mph faster than the Zeke 52
At 5,000 ft the FM-2 was 4 mph slower than the Zeke 52
At 10,000 ft the FM-2 was 12 mph slower than the Zeke 52
At 15,000 ft the FM-2 was 8 mph slower than the Zeke 52
At 20,000 ft the FM-2 was 19 mph slower than the Zeke 52
At 25,000 ft the FM-2 was 22 mph slower than the Zeke 52
At 30,000 ft the FM-2 was 26 mph slower than the Zeke 52

Top speeds attained were 321 mph at 13,000 feet for the FM-2 and 335 mph at 18,000 feet for the Zeke 52.

Climb. The best climb of the Zeke 52 was about 400 ft/min less than that of the FM-2 at sea-level, became equal at about 4,000 feet, was 500 ft/min better at 8,000 feet, became equal again at 13,000 feet, and was only slightly inferior above 13,000 feet. The best climbing speeds for the FM-2 and the Zeke 52 were found to be 140 mph and 123 mph, respectively.

Dive. The Zeke 52 was slightly superior to the FM-2 in initial dive acceleration, after which the dives were about the same. Zooms after dives were about equal for the Zeke 52 and the FM-2.

Turning circle. The turns of the FM-2 and the Zeke 52 were very similar, with a slight advantage in favour of the Zeke 52. The Zeke 52 could gain one turn in eight at 10,000 feet.

Rate of roll. The roll of the Zeke 52 was equal to that of the FM-2 at speeds under 178 mph, and inferior above that speed, due to the high control forces.

Manoeuvrability. The manoeuvrability of the Zeke 52 is remarkable at speeds below 205 mph, being slightly superior to the FM-2. Its slight superiority, however, decreases with increased speeds, due to its high control forces, and the FM-2 has the advantage at speeds above 235 mph.

Vision. As for the F6F-5.

Conclusions. Do not dog-fight with the Zeke 52. Maintain any altitude advantage you may have. To evade a Zeke 52 on your tail, roll and dive away into a high speed turn.

Zeke 52 versus Seafire L IIC

Maximum speed. The Seafire L IIC was faster below about 17,000 feet; the Zeke 52 was faster above that altitude.

At sea level the Seafire L IIC was 24 mph faster than the Zeke 52
At 5,000 ft the Seafire L IIC was 24 mph faster than the Zeke 52
At 10,000 ft the Seafire L IIC was 18 mph faster than the Zeke 52
At 15,000 ft the Seafire L IIC was 8 mph faster than the Zeke 52
At 20,000 ft the Seafire L IIC was 5 mph slower than the Zeke 52
At 25,000 feet the Seafire L IIC was 10 mph slower than the Zeke 52.

Top speeds attained were 338 mph at 5,500 feet for the Seafire L IIC and 335 mph at 18,000 feet for the Zeke 52.

Climb. The Zeke 52 climbs at a very steep angle and gives an impression of a very high rate of climb. The Seafire L IIC, however, has a much better initial climb and remains slightly superior up to 25,000 feet. The climb of the Seafire is at a faster speed, but a more shallow angle. The best climbing speeds for the Seafire and Zeke 52 were 160 and 123 mph respectively.

Dive. The Seafire is superior in the dive although initial acceleration is similar. The Zeke is a most unpleasant aircraft in a dive, due to heavy stick forces and excessive vibration.

Turning circle. The Zeke 52 can turn inside the Seafire L IIC at all heights.

Rate of roll. The rate of roll of the two aircraft is similar at speeds below 180 mph indicated, but above that the aileron stick forces of the Zeke increase tremendously, and the Seafire becomes progressively superior.

Conclusions. Never dog-fight with a Zeke 52 – it is too manoeuvrable. At low altitudes where the Seafire is at its best, it should make use of its superior rate of climb and speed to obtain a height advantage before attacking. If jumped, the Seafire should evade by using its superior rate of roll. The Zeke cannot follow high speed rolls and aileron turns.

Hook down ready, a Seafire LIIC is seen about to touch down on the deck of an escort carrier. Powered by a 1,640 horse-power Merlin 32, this fighter had a maximum speed of 338 mph at 5,500 feet and had clipped wings for optimum low level performance. With an armament of two 20-mm and four .303-inch machine guns, the loaded weight was 7,000 pounds. Developed from the Spitfire, the Seafire was the only landplane modified for carrier operations to see large-scale naval service during the war; and all too frequently its undercarriage proved too weak for deck landings. The Mark I and II Seafires did not have folding wings, though later versions did. *via Brown*

Werner Moelders,
second from left, the
leading German
fighter ace of the early
war period, explaining
a tactical point to
three of his brother
officers.
via Schliephake

3 The Tactics of Battle.

*The art of war consists in always having more
forces than the adversary, even with an army weaker
than his, at the point where one is attacking
or being attacked.*

NAPOLEON

*Nine-tenths of tactics are certain,
and taught in books; but the irrational
tenth is like the kingfisher flashing across the pool,
and that is the test of generals.*

T. E. LAWRENCE

When the Second World War began, few air forces had a clear idea of what their fighters could accomplish. The engagement of enemy bombers was their primary task, though what degree of success they would have had still to be proven. And would they be required to engage enemy fighters? Many experts believed that the increase in performance of fighters since 1918 had made dogfighting a thing of the past. The Royal Air Force Manual of Air Tactics, 1938 edition, solemnly stated:

Manoeuvre at high speeds in air fighting is not now practicable, because the effect of gravity on the human body during rapid changes of direction at high speed causes a temporary loss of consciousness, deflection shooting becomes difficult and accuracy is hard to obtain.

As a result of this line of thinking, there arose a set of fighter tactics designed solely for use against enemy bombers. The possibility of fighter-versus-fighter combat was almost ignored.

In the bomber formations in general use during the 1930s, the usual element was a V of three aircraft; it was considered, therefore, that the optimum fighter element to engage them was a section of three fighters. To take the Royal Air Force as an example, the cruising formation for a twelve aircraft fighter squadron comprised four Vs, each V consisting of a section of three aircraft. The squadron commander flew in the middle of the leading V, and the other three Vs flew behind in close line astern. The fighters flew very close together with about one wing span, 12 yards, between them. This type of close formation was chosen because it was considered the best for the penetration of cloud, an important factor to be considered in air operations over northern Europe.

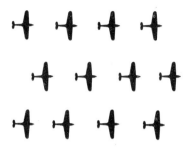

RAF Squadron formation, early war period; to scale.

The squadron commander was to lead his formation to a position on the flank of the enemy bomber formation. Once there he ordered his sections into echelon, and took his own section in to attack. The aim of each fighter pilot was to get into a firing position behind an enemy bomber where (in the words of the 1938 RAF Manual of Air Tactics) '. . . he stays until either he has exhausted his ammunition, the target aircraft has been shot down, or he himself has been shot down or his engine put out of action'. The other sections were to queue up behind and attack after the section in front had broken away.

The tactical formation and type of attack outlined above were not the only ones in use in the Royal Air Force. They can, however, be considered representative of the rigidity of tactical thinking not only in that air force but in many others prior to the war.

In 1939 the only evidence available to most air forces on the nature of modern air warfare was that they had been able to glean from the mass of conflicting reports, often tinged with propaganda, from the Spanish civil war. In a sense studying such reports was like perusing the Bible: no matter what one was trying to prove, one was almost certain to find evidence to support it. The civil war had shown that the bombers almost always did get through, and they were able to cause severe damage to built-up areas. There had been a lot of fighter-versus-fighter combat, but much of it had been inconclusive and relatively little of it had been between monoplane fighters of modern design.

Only in Germany were the lessons of the Spanish civil war, many of them learnt at first hand, put to good use. The Luftwaffe fighter pilots returned from the conflict with no doubts that air combat between modern fighters, though difficult, was possible and almost certain in any future war. In Spain Leutnant Werner Moelders, one of the top scorers of the conflict with 14 victories, had experimented with a new set of tactics for fighters based on the *Rotte*, or widely-spaced pair of aircraft. During cruising flight the two aircraft flew almost in line abreast, the leader slightly ahead, about 200

RAF Squadron in attack.

yards apart; each pilot concentrated his search inwards, so that he covered his partner's blind areas behind and below. In combat against enemy fighters, it was the wing-man's duty to guard his leader's tail while the latter did the fighting; when attacking unescorted bombers, the leader picked a target and the wing-man engaged the aircraft next to it.

Two *Rotten* made up a *Schwarm* of four aircraft, with the leading *Rotte*

Werner Moelders was largely responsible for evolving the successful German *Rotte* and *Schwarm* tactics, which came to be adopted by other air forces as the war progressed.

flying to one side and slightly ahead of the other, and the aircraft were stepped down into the sun. With its component aircraft spaced about 200 yards apart the *Schwarm* formation was approximately 600 yards wide, which made it almost impossible for the aircraft to hold position during a tight turn at high speed. Moelders solved this problem with the 'cross-over' turn, in which all aircraft turned as tightly as they could and simply swapped sides in the formation. A *Staffel* battle formation comprised twelve fighters in three *Schwaerme* either in line astern or in line abreast.

Moelders had evolved his tactics with fighter-versus-fighter combat in mind but, such was their flexibility, the fighters could simply close up and be as effective as the tight RAF formation when it came to penetrating cloud or attacking unescorted bombers. In determining the effectiveness of a combat formation for fighters, three factors need to be considered:

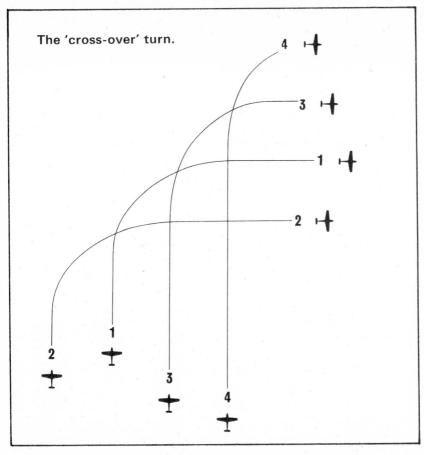

The 'cross-over' turn.

first, the ability of the aircraft in the formation to manoeuvre as required yet still maintain cohesion; secondly, the ability of the pilots to search each others' blind areas and thus prevent a surprise attack on any of the aircraft; and thirdly, the ability of each of the aircraft in the formation to receive rapid support from one or more of the others if it came under attack. On each of these three criteria, the German tactical formations were greatly superior to the tight formations in use in the RAF and other air forces. Using the 'cross-over' turn, the *Schwarm* could turn as tightly as its component aircraft were able and the same went for the *Staffel*; in the tight formation of Vs, the leader was forced to slacken his turn to allow for the minimum turning radius possible for the men on the inside. During cruising flight the *Schwarm* was so fluid that every pilot could concentrate on searching the sky for the enemy, and each man was well positioned to cover his comrades' blind areas; in the tight formation of Vs only the squadron commander could spend all of his time looking out for the enemy, as his men were most of the time busy concentrating on holding their position in the formation – with the result that there was poor coverage of the all-important rear sector. If an aircraft in a *Rotte* or *Schwarm* was attacked from behind, a simple turn could result in the attacker being 'sandwiched';

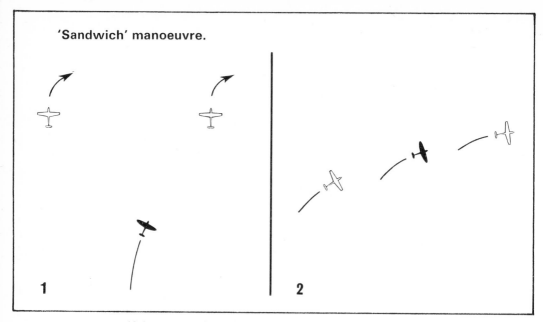

'Sandwich' manoeuvre.

1

2

if the rear section of a tight formation of Vs was attacked from behind, the action was usually over before it could receive any help from any of the other sections.

In May 1940 the Germans launched their great offensive into France and Belgium, and the war in the air began in earnest. It was not long before the shortcomings of the Royal Air Force fighter tactics were revealed in combat. At that time Flying Officer Roland Beaumont was flying Hurricanes with No 87 Squadron in France and he later recalled of one of the early actions:

We were operating from a grass field at Lille Marque and had been ordered off at three squadron strength to patrol the ground battle area at Valencienne at 10,000 feet.

We made a fine sight as 36 Hurricanes formed up in the late afternoon sun in three squadrons in line astern, with four sections of Vic threes to a squadron.

I was flying No. 2 to the right of the commander of No. 87 Squadron who was leading the wing, and it made one feel quite brave looking back at so many friendly fighters. Then, without fuss or drama, about ten Messerschmitt 109s appeared above the left rear flank of our formation out of some high cloud.

The Wing Leader turned in towards them as fast as the big formation could be wheeled, but the 109s abandoned close drill and pulled their turn tight, dived one after the other on to the tail sections of the wing. Their guns streamed smoke and one by one four Hurricanes fell away. None of us fired a shot, some never even saw it happen, and the enemy disengaged while we continued to give a massive impression of combat strength over the battle area with four less Hurricanes than we had started.

We had more than three times the strength of the enemy on this occasion and had been soundly beaten tactically by a much smaller unit led with flexibility and resolution.

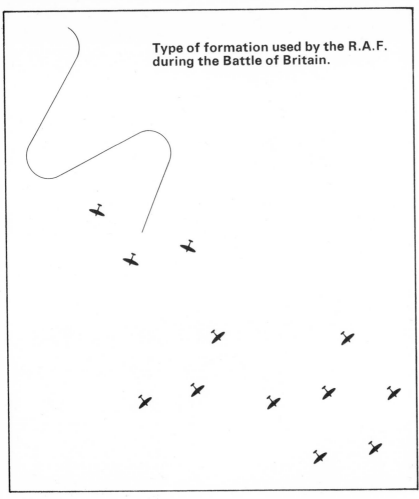

Type of formation used by the R.A.F. during the Battle of Britain.

During the weeks that followed there were scores of similar incidents and it became clear that the Royal Air Force fighter tactics were quite inadequate for the type of war now in progress. But by then the Battle of Britain was about to begin and there simply was no time for a complete change of tactics. On paper the *Schwarm* formation looks simple enough, but pilots needed considerable practice to accustom themselves to its use and get the most out of it. The Royal Air Force would have to fight its decisive battle making the most of the inflexible tactics in which its fighter pilots had been trained. The V formation was widened out slightly, so that the pilots could spend more time searching for the enemy rather than holding an exact distance from their neighbours; and one section, led by an experienced pilot, was stationed about 1,000 feet above the formation flying a weaving course and keeping watch for the enemy. These two steps greatly improved the search and mutual support capabilities of the fighter squadrons, though they did little to improve the main formation's ability to manoeuvre with cohesion.

'Sailor' Malan, who, as commander of No 74 Squadron, worked out a tactical system much used in the Royal Air Force during the mid-war period. *I.W.M.*

By the close of the Battle of Britain many different types of battle formation were in use in RAF Fighter Command. Some squadrons used the single weaving section described above; other squadrons used two separate weaving aircraft; other squadrons still experimented with two separate flights each with a weaving aircraft; yet others employed six loose pairs of aircraft.

Malan's formation, to scale.

It was at this time that Squadron Leader 'Sailor' Malan, commanding No 74 Squadron, made his mark on the tactical scene. Instead of the earlier division of the squadron into four sections each of three aircraft, Malan split his unit into three sections each of four aircraft. This was an important change, because when the mêlée began and the formation broke up the four-aircraft sections split easily into two fighting units each of two aircraft. Malan's theory was that a three-aircraft fighting unit contained one too many; and a lone fighter in the combat area was a potential sitting duck. Malan arranged his squadron with the sections in a loose V, each with its aircraft in line astern.

By the three criteria for an effective fighter formation, manoeuvrability with cohesion, coverage of blind areas and mutual support, this type of formation was a great improvement over any of the others in use in the RAF during the Battle of Britain. When a tight turn was required, the section leaders went into a 'cross over' turn and the aircraft behind simply followed. Since the loose line astern formation was easy to fly there was plenty of time for all pilots to search for the enemy, and they were well positioned to cover each others' blind areas. With the sections spaced 200 to 300 yards apart, it was a simple matter to 'sandwich' an attacker behind any one of them. The value of Malan's formation was quickly recognised, and from the end of the Battle of Britain until well into 1943 it was the one most used in the Royal Air Force.

Malan's formation worked well enough for RAF Fighter Command, which during 1941 and 1942 used it during the large-scale offensive sweeps over Belgium and northern France. In the Middle East, and in particular over Malta, it was a different story, however; there the Allies had far fewer aircraft and fighters often had to go into action in units of less than twelve. Under such conditions Malan's formation was not suitable. The German *Rotte* and *Schwarm* formations held distinct advantages, and came gradually to be copied by RAF squadrons. At the same time the tendency developed

Reade Tilley, pictured as a Major in the U.S.A.A.F. in 1943. As a Flying Officer in the Royal Air Force he had flown Spitfires over Malta, and he set down many of the lessons learnt in his tactical paper 'Hints on Hun Hunting'. *Tilley.*

to fly the *Schwarm* with the four aircraft flattened out until they were almost in line abreast. This had the advantage that to hold formation each pilot had to be looking inwards towards his leader, which meant that the search for the enemy was automatically concentrated in the blind areas of the other aircraft.

By the end of 1943 the basic German *Rotte* and *Schwarm* tactics were in use in all the major air forces. In the Royal Air Force and the U.S. Army Air Force they were known respectively as the pair and finger-four; to the Japanese they were the *Buntai* and the *Shotai*; to the Russians they were known as the *Para* and *Zveno*.

A good tactical formation was essential if fighters were to operate effectively against their enemy counterparts, but there were other things that were almost as important. Reade Tilley was an American who joined the Royal Air Force before his country entered the war and served with No 121 'Eagle' Squadron. Early in 1942 he went to Malta, and flew Spitfires during the hard-fought battles over that besieged island in the spring and summer; he was credited with the destruction of seven enemy aircraft. At the end of the year he transferred to the U.S.A.A.F. with the rank of Captain and was sent to a fighter training unit to pass on his experience to new pilots. Early in 1943 he set down the lessons he had learned in a tactical paper entitled 'Hints on Hun Hunting', excerpts of which are given below. It provides an insight into the qualities that were required to survive as a fighter pilot in a war zone where the enemy frequently held superiority; if some of the points are made dramatically, it should be remembered that Tilley served his apprenticeship in a pitiless school where death often came swiftly to those who failed to learn, or to observe, the lessons of combat. He opened his treatise with a series of dos and don'ts for the take-off and climb away from base.

Spitfire Vs of Tilley's unit, No 126 Squadron, at cockpit readiness at Luqa, Malta, in the summer of 1942. *C. R. Long*

When fighters are scrambled to intercept an approaching enemy, every minute wasted in getting off the ground and forming up means 3,000 feet of altitude you won't have when you need it most. Thus an elaborate cockpit check is out. It is sufficient to see that you are in fine pitch and the motor is running properly before opening the throttle. Don't do a Training School circuit before joining up. As you roll down the runway take a quick look up for the man off ahead of you, when you have sufficient indicated air speed give him about six rings of deflection [of the gunsight] and you will be alongside in a flash. Don't jam open the throttle and follow along behind as it takes three times as long to catch up that way. If you are leading circle the drome close in, throttled well back, waggling your wings like Hell.

The instant you are in formation get the cockpit in 'fighting shape': trimmed for the climb, oxygen right, check engine instruments, gun button to fire. Now you are ready for action. If something is wrong *now* is the time to go back. Waggle your wings then slide gently out of the formation, or if following break sharply down and go home. *Never* wait until you are in the vicinity of enemy aircraft then make a break for it on a last minute decision. There are several reasons, ie:

A. The leader may be depending on you.
B. The rest of the formation may think you are diving on the enemy and follow you (this has happened plenty of times and it plays Hell with everything).
C. The enemy may spot you and take advantage of your solitude.

Tilley set great store by the 'fours line abreast' formation, a variation of the basic *Schwarm*. Although the aircraft are shown in exact line abreast there was a tendency for the leader to be slightly in front; woe betide any fighter pilot who edged in front of his formation leader!

The formation that has proved its worth in both offensive and defensive fighter operations is the 'fours line abreast'. The following diagram explains it—the squadron is divided into three sections, aircraft flying 200 to 250 yards apart.

Fours in line abreast.

Red Section leads, with the squadron commander at Red 1. Red 3, the second in command, flies next to the squadron commander on his left; he will take over the lead in case the squadron commander's radio fails or he has to leave the squadron because his aircraft is unserviceable. On the signal Red 3 will open up and forge ahead meaning he understands and has taken over.
The usual form in obsolete formations has been to have the second in command leading a separate section usually well behind, so far in fact that he frequently missed the signal to take over or left the squadron without a leader for a few minutes while he moved into position in the lead. There was also confusion when his own section tried to follow him to the front.

White and Blue Sections fly 500 to 800 yards behind the one side and slightly above the Red Section. The individual aircraft fly 5 to 7 spans [60 to 85 yards] apart. When the leader turns, White and Blue Sections will cross over at full throttle. The section the leader turns towards will usually cross under, the other over. In order to be in position when the turn is completed, the leaders of White and Blue Sections have to be quick and precise. Within the sections each pilot will cross over. The first pilot to feel uncomfortable holding his position will initiate the cross over and when he starts all must cross over.

Squadron commanders must bear in mind that the squadron must be intact to do maximum damage to the enemy in combat; to this end throttle back and even turn towards straggling sections while climbing to meet the enemy. There is no better feeling than to arrive at 25,000 feet with the full squadron properly deployed and then start hunting.

In section 'fours line abreast' each aircraft watches the others' tails, above and below; and in doing so all four cover each other:

Section of four aircraft giving mutual cover, to scale.
(*Shading indicates blind zones.*)

The arrows indicate the direction in which the pilots keep watch. When everyone does his job it is impossible for enemy aircraft to get into a firing position without being seen by at least three out of the four pilots. On a larger scale the sections cover each other. Any one section that is being attacked will be covered by the next section; and the pay off is that the enemy frequently sees only one or two sections, and in attacking or manoeuvring lay themselves wide open to the attentions of the third section.

One further advantage of this formation is that if one man is attacked the man next to him is at the exact distance where he can throttle back and fire at the attacker from the beam. Moreover, the sections are at the exact distance apart so that they are in effective range of any aircraft who is within range astern of one of the others.

For the sort of co-ordinated fighter operations which have been described, good radio communications were essential. Without a radio a fighter pilot was both deaf and dumb, a liability to himself and his comrades. Yet even worse than that, as Tilley pointed out, was a fighter pilot who used his radio wantonly or thoughtlessly.

Forget all the fancy pleasantries you learned to put before and after the message in voice radio procedure. In your business there is no time for it and the message is the important thing. The squadron leader is the only man who uses the RT for transmission when the squadron is in pursuit of the German. There is no need for you to say anything, just keep your mouth

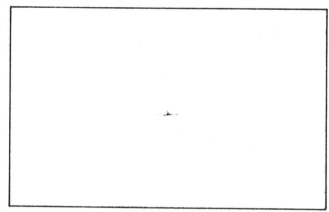

In the words of the top-scoring Malta ace, the Canadian Squadron Leader 'Screwball' Beurling, 'The flyers who see first usually shoot first, for they have already won half the battle.' To see the enemy first demanded a systematic search and unflagging concentration from a fighter pilot the whole time he was in the combat area; the slightest lapse could be, and often was, fatal. This photograph, held 18 inches from the eye, gives an idea of the magnitude of the problem. A fighter at 600 yards, just about to open fire; if it has managed to get into position behind at this range without being seen, unless the enemy pilot's shooting was bad, it would probably be too late to do anything.

shut and reflect on the ground controller's messages to the leader. You will learn all you need to know: how many of the enemy to expect, at what altitude and from what direction they are approaching. The leader acknowledges messages from the ground controller with a sharp 'OK'. That is all that is necessary unless several squadrons or sections are operating independently, in which case 'Red Leader OK' or 'Blue Leader answering OK' is sufficient. The latter message takes $2\frac{1}{2}$ seconds; until the enemy is sighted no transmission should be longer. If a 4- or 5-second message about nothing in particular is in progress, when everyone suddenly realises that the wing man is being fired at by a Focke Wulf, then no one can warn him till the message is completed and he probably won't be interested by then. It's amazing how many holes can be punched in an airplane in four or five seconds. . . .

So keep your eyes open and your mouth shut until you spot the enemy, then your moment has come. If they are far ahead, or off to one side or below and far away from you, there is plenty of time; don't get excited, just sit there and look them over – it doesn't help much if you report Spitfires as 109s. Try to count them or make a rapid estimate (for your log book). If you recognise them give their identity; if not, report them as 'aircraft'. The procedure: make your voice purposely calm, slow and unexcited: 'Hello Red Leader; 109s at 4 o'clock above' or 'Red 3 to Red Leader; aircraft at 9 o'clock our level'.

Red Leader sees the aircraft and acknowledges 'OK'. Now above all leave the RT clear, for the next words will be your leader's instruction. If these are jammed it may queer the whole set-up.

Sometimes enemy aircraft are not seen until they are actually attacking. *Then the message must be instantaneous and precise.* If it is incoherent or garbled because you are excited the man being attacked may get a cannon shell instead – and first. The proper procedure: '109s attacking Red Section' or if you see one man being fired at 'Look out Red 4' or 'Red 4 break'; any one of these messages spoken clearly is perfect. Just be sure you designate the man being attacked correctly. It doesn't help much if you tell Red 4 to break (which he does) while Red 2, who is being fired at, looks on admiringly.

The one sure way to lose friends and help the enemy is to give a panic message over the RT at the critical moment. 'Look out, there's a 109 on your tail!', said in a screech, is usually sufficient to send every Spitfire within a radius of 50 miles into a series of wild manoeuvres. There is no call sign used so every pilot in every squadron responds automatically. Far better to say nothing at all and let one pilot be shot down than to break up several formations for Jerry to pick off at his leisure. In fighter flying a panic message is the greatest of all crimes. Practice on the ground the exact words you will use to cover any situation in the air; say them over and over again until they become automatic. If your RT packs up near base, go back; if near the enemy, stay with the squadron. A fighter pilot without RT is a liability to himself and his squadron. Never taken off with a faulty RT.

For the fighter pilot, the sun could be either a powerful ally or a deadly foe. Which one, depended on how well the pilot used its protection and guarded the sector in which it lay.

Always note the bearing of the sun before taking off; then, if you get in a scrap miles out at sea or over the desert and a cannon shell prangs your compass, you may be able to save yourself a lot of unnecessary walking or paddling.

Never climb down sun. If it is necessary to fly down sun, do so in a series of 45 degree tacks. If circumstances permit, always climb up sun. If a German is hiding in it, he can make only one head-on pass at you, then you can turn smartly and jump him out of the sun thus foxing him at his own game.

If you are patrolling an objective, split your force into two sections and patrol across sun. The sections will fly more or less line abreast, but with the up-sun section out in front just a bit. Vary the length of the legs you cover and gain and lose altitude all the while. If the Germans spot you first, this will make it more difficult for them to time an attack to get you on the turn; and always make the turns *into* sun.

When stalking the wily Hun, bear in mind that he seldom puts all his eggs in one bucket but usually splits his aircraft into several groups, each group stacked up-sun, three to five thousand feet. Keep an eye on the sun; you will be safer. The Germans are masters at using stooge decoys who would probably be as helpless as they look, if half the Luftwaffe was not keeping a jealous eye on them from the sun.

Cloud, too, could prove a friend or a foe depending on how it was used.

Cloud is greatly over-rated as cover for offensive fighter operations. It is of most use to a fighter pilot who is in trouble. If you are shot up or the odds are impossible, it is great stuff to hide in. Layer cloud is most useful as you can pop in, or dive out below to take a look. Remember that it is not healthy to maintain a straight course when there are gaps in the cloud. If you are being pursued turn 90 degrees in every cloud you pop into; if it seems in order, a quick 180 about may put you in a position to offer some head-on discouragement to the pursuer along the way.

Never fly directly on top of layer cloud, as you stand out like a sore thumb to an unfriendly element, even those as far as 10 miles away, if they are slightly above you. It is no use to play hide and seek in amongst the clouds when you are hunting for 109s. You get a tremendously safe feeling in amongst the white stuff and expect an enemy to pop out directly in your sights at any moment; actually it is very dangerous, because you are silhouetted in all directions and he will see you first, then take mean advantage of your cover and your posterior.

On days when there is very high layer cloud, fly half way between it and the ground in order to spot fighters above you. High layer cloud is perfect for defensive fighter work, because you can see the enemy formations and distinguish between fighter and bomber long before they can see you.

The next stage to be discussed was the *raison d'être* for the fighter: the combat. Usually it was short and sharp, and always it was fraught with perils for the unwary.

German top cover is usually at 28,000 feet, though it may be as high as 32,000 feet. When you attain maximum altitude, you will have an even break with the small number of enemy aircraft usually employed as top cover. If they are sighted it is better to detach an equal number to deal with them; then you can tackle the main force, more or less confident that you will have no unwelcome attentions from above. Remember, regardless of where or when you go in to attack an enemy formation, if at all possible leave two or four aircraft to cover you from above.

Enemy aircraft do not fly alone, they fly in pairs or fours. If you can see just one, have a damn good look round for his pal before you go in to attack . . . and remember, *look out behind!*

When you attack, a series of two or three second bursts with new aim and angle of deflection each time is most effective. Don't cease attacking just because the enemy aircraft is beginning to smoke or a few pieces fall off; then is the time to skid out for a good look behind, before closing in to point blank range and really giving it to him.

When actually firing at the enemy aircraft you are most vulnerable to attack. When you break away from an attack *always* break with a violent skid just as though you were being fired at from behind – because maybe you are!

It would seem reasonable to suppose that the straggler in a fighter formation would be the last man to get home; but he rarely is! Play hard to get, don't straggle, *and look out behind, always!*

The first action after combat is not to shake hands with yourself but to look at the engine instruments. Dropping oil pressure and rising engine and oil temperatures mean trouble. If you have been hit in the radiator or in the glycol pipes white smoke starts to flow immediately. This is usually visible from the cockpit. If you have had bad luck the main glycol feed pipe running alongside the cockpit may be ruptured, in which case the cockpit will be filled with hot glycol and dense white vapour which causes choking and blindness. There is no hope to save an aircraft so hit. If, however, the glycol smoke is outside open the hood, turn the oxygen on to emergency and land at the nearest drome. If you have a long way to go to reach your lines or coast, throttle well back in coarse pitch and prepare to get out or crash land should the engine quit.

A hit through the oil piping or motor block is not so obvious though it will show on your oil pressure and engine instruments immediately. Often it is possible to cover a good many miles well throttled back in coarse pitch before the engine seizes. When your aircraft starts trailing heavy smoke it may catch fire at any moment so watch for the first sign of flame; if it appears, bail out immediately as an explosion may follow without further warning.

The only way you can't get out of a Spitfire is to climb out. The best method, if you have time, is to roll over on your back, trim her a bit tail heavy then pull the pin [holding together the seat harness] and fall clear. If you are in a hurry (and sometimes this is the case), just pull the pin and jam the stick forward; your last sensation will be your fingers leaving the stick. This works with the aircraft in any position. If the hood is jammed shut and you can't open it (sometimes a bullet or a shell may foul the track) lower the seat to the bottom, pull the pin, stiffen the neck and back muscles, then give the stick one Hell of a shove forward. You won't even notice the hood . . .

Look out behind, then all of this won't be necessary.

One point omitted from Tilley's paper, which some may consider significant, was guidance on standard aerobatic manoeuvres for use in combat. The reason was that they were, for the most part, irrelevant. The art of fighter-versus-fighter combat was to see the enemy first, get into a position of advantage above and preferably up-sun of him, then dive into the attack and hope to announce one's presence with a lethal burst. If the attackers were seen in time, their opponents would try to turn to meet them and thus nullify the attack. If there was no time to turn to meet the attack, the attacked formation would usually split into pairs and what followed next

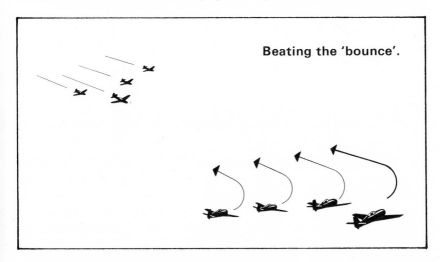

Beating the 'bounce'.

most often depended upon the types of aircraft involved. Tilley was flying the Spitfire which was able to out-turn the German fighters it met in combat; therefore in the Spitfire, and in the Russian and Japanese fighters which were also more manoeuvrable than their adversaries, the usual evasive manoeuvre was the hardest possible turn into the direction of the attack sometimes combined with a slight climb which greatly increased the difficulties of deflection shooting. For those aircraft that were less manoeuvrable than their attackers, however, to continue in such a turning fight would have been tantamount to committing suicide; but these aircraft were usually faster, especially in the dive, so their pilots would often adopt the manoeuvre known in the Royal Air Force as the half-roll, in the U.S.A.A.F. as the Split-S and in the Luftwaffe as the *Abschwung*. The pilot pushed his throttle wide open, rolled over on to his back, and pulled back on the stick until the fighter was in a near vertical power dive. The speed built up very rapidly, though at a cost in altitude that might be as much as 10,000 feet, and was usually effective in shaking off a pursuer with a worse diving performance.

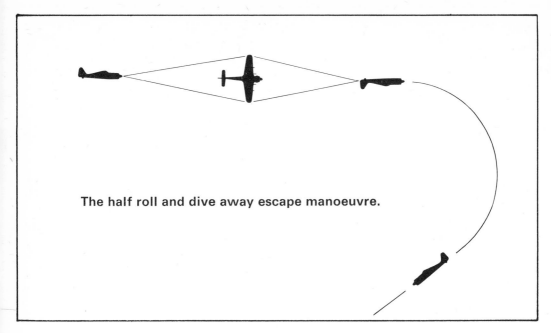

The half roll and dive away escape manoeuvre.

An escape manoeuvre often used by twin-engined fighters was that known in the Royal Air Force as the defensive circle, in the U.S.A.A.F. as the Lufbery (after the American First World War ace who pioneered its use) and in the Luftwaffe as the *Abwehrkreis*. The fighters in the attacked formation pulled round into a circle so that each was guarding the tail of the one in front. The idea was that no attacker could spend long on anybody's tail without himself coming under fire from behind. Its use by twin-engined fighters was usually dictated by their lack of the necessary turning or diving performance to succeed with other escape manoeuvres; however, these aircraft usually had the advantage of sufficient endurance to be able to hang around until their attackers ran short of fuel and had to break away.

An example of the successful use of the defensive circle is to be found in the diary of the U.S. Army Air Force 49th Fighter Squadron for June 14th 1944. On that day fifteen of the unit's P-38 Lightnings were taking part in a bomber escort mission over Hungary when they came under attack by an estimated fifty enemy fighters. First Lieutenant Thomas Purdy, who led one of the Flights, afterwards reported:

Just as the last wave of bombers was over the target we were jumped from 4 o'clock; they were in two big bunches and attacked us from both sides simultaneously. Our squadron leader called 'Hangman drop tanks, break right'. I was leading White Flight which was directly to the left of the squadron leader's flight, when Red Flight broke right. I saw enemy aircraft attacking them from the rear. I immediately broke to the left. White Flight got there in the nick of time to ward off the attack on Red Flight's tail. I damaged one Me 109 and three other Me's went down. Blue Flight also broke to the left and Green Flight broke to the right. Thus we set up two 'Lufberys', one to the left and the other to the right.

Jerry was all over us. They were in and out of our squadron continuously. I saw one P-38 spin down out of the formation because we were turning so sharply. He stalled out and lost some altitude. Two Me's were on his tail, shooting all they had at him. I went down and shot one down as I saw him burst into flames; the other Split-S'd when he saw my tracers around him. This P-38 got back into the 'Lufbery' a few minutes later. I saw one P-38 blow up. He was in a straight glide, both engines blazing, leaving long flaming trails behind him. I called and said: 'P-38 on fire, bail out.' No response was received.

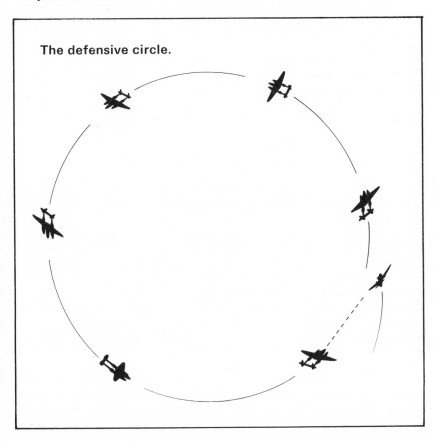

The defensive circle.

From then on all we did was continue circling in 'Lufberys', chasing Me 109s off each other's tails. There wasn't one split moment went by that I couldn't see Me's in front, above, beside and below, they came from above and every direction. One got in behind my flight and luckily put only one hit on one of my propellers. I then saw two Me's on another P-38. The P-38 was flying level and away from the 'Lufbery'. I turned and sprayed tracers around them; one immediately Split-S'd, but the other kept shooting at the P-38. I then closed in and shot his tail assembly completely off; he went straight down. At the same time this P-38 was streaming out white-grey smoke and starting a long straight dive. I called and told him to bail out, but there was no response.

We were all using plenty of ammunition, no one realising it. I figured it was a fight to the finish and let it go at that. This carried on for at least 25 minutes and then came a lull in the battle. I looked up to see some 25 Me's above us; and there were only a few still making passes at us. Someone said 'Purdy, let's make a run for it.' I turned to the right out of the 'Lufbery' making steep sharp turns to left and right. We had to break right as two Me's were attacking from the rear. They went down and we headed south again, weaving violently one way, then the other. I could see only seven P-38s following me.

During the mêlée the 49th Fighter Squadron lost five aircraft; its pilots claimed thirteen of the enemy shot down and a further five damaged, though in view of the ferocity of the engagement this was probably an overclaim. There is evidence that the attackers belonged to the Hungarian 101st Fighter Regiment, which was equipped with Messerschmitt 109Gs; during a home defence mission that day the Hungarian ace György Debrödy was credited with shooting down a P-38. But the main point was that two-thirds of the American fighters had been able to survive a protracted battle with a greatly superior number of faster and more manoeuvrable enemy fighters.

Sometimes, however, the defensive circle could prove a death trap for those who used it. On occasions during the Battle of Britain, RAF single-engined fighters succeeded in getting into defensive circles of Messerschmitt 110s; by flying round the inside of the enemy circle in the opposite direction, it was possible to engage each aircraft in turn, without their being above to bring their fixed armament to bear. Also, there is the well-authenticated story of the German fighter ace Hans Joachim Marseille, who on June 6th 1942 over Libya by himself shot down six P-40 Tomahawk fighters of No 5 Squadron South African Air Force, which had been flying in a defensive circle. Marseille's tactics were to choose a victim in the circle and dive on it from above, and he was so good at judging the angles of deflection that he could knock his enemy out of the sky with one quick burst before the fighter guarding its tail could engage him; after each such attack the German ace zoomed back above the circling enemy fighters and positioned himself for his next attack.

So much for fighter-versus-fighter tactics. Those against unescorted medium or light bombers were usually straightforward, and summed up by the adage 'Never mind the tactics, get at 'em'. The main difficulty against such targets was usually confined to making contact and getting into a firing position, particularly in the case of the high speed types over which the fighters had little margin in speed. Medium and light bombers rarely carried sufficient defensive armament to present any serious problems for determined fighter pilots.

From mid-1942 an entirely new problem emerged for the German and Japanese fighter pilots: the heavily-armed and armoured American four-engined bomber. These aircraft, B-17s and B-24s, each carried a defensive armament of ten or more .5-inch heavy machine guns; and they flew in tight formations of eighteen or more aircraft so that each was able to receive the protection of covering fire from its neighbours. Initially the German and Japanese fighters were too lightly armed to engage in slugging matches with these formations, though they were soon modified to carry heavy cannon to enable them to do so.

Most of the attacks on the heavy bombers were made from the rear hemisphere; but for the pilots who were able to shoot straight, the head-on attack held several advantages. Not only was there far lower risk of the fighter being hit during its run-in, since fewer of the defensive guns could be brought to bear and there was less time for them to fire, but the armour protection for the bomber crewmen behind and beneath their positions gave no cover against attacks from the front. The standard German head-on attack, to take an example, began with the fighters making contact with

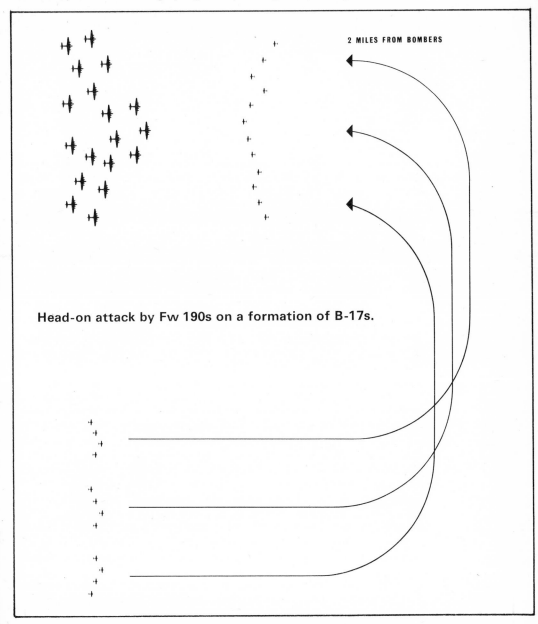

2 MILES FROM BOMBERS

Head-on attack by Fw 190s on a formation of B-17s.

Johann Pichler, right, pictured beside the Messerschmitt 109G he flew with such success against the American heavy bombers. *Pichler*

the bombers and trailing them for a short time while the fighter leader gauged their course and speed. That done, he took his fighters past the bombers outside the range of the defensive fire to a position about two miles in front; then the fighter *Schwaerme* did cross-over turns through a semi-circle and rolled out into near line-abreast for their attack. Since the bombers cruised at about 175 mph and the German fighters attacked at speeds around 300 mph, the closing speed was nearly 500 mph. If their pilots opened fire at 700 yards there was time for a maximum of only about 2 seconds firing before they had to break off the attack. When they had finished firing the better German pilots pulled up to pass close overhead the bombers they had aimed at; this prevented their being hit by falling debris from the target, while at the same time allowing the defensive gunners little chance of scoring a lethal burst during the time they were at short range.

One of the leading German exponents of the head-on attack on heavy bomber formations was Johann Pichler, who flew Messerschmitt 109Gs with the *III Gruppe* of *Jagdgeschwader 77* based in Rumania. Although his aircraft carried an armament of only three 20-mm cannon and two 13-mm machine guns, insufficient for the average pilot to achieve much against such targets, before his capture in August 1944 Pichler had shot down seven B-17s and seven B-24s. Pichler attributed his success to a sharp eye and a cool head; during his head-on attacks he withheld his fire until he was sure of hitting, then a 1 or 1½ second burst was usually sufficient. He always aimed at the cockpit. 'The cockpit is the "brain" of the aircraft,' he later recalled, 'once it has been hit with two or three cannon shells the bomber is definitely out of action'. Other, less capable pilots in Pichler's *Gruppe* opened fire at maximum range and continued until they broke away and afterwards insisted that they had pumped the bombers full of shells but the latter had refused to go down. 'Nonsense', was Pichler's usual reply, 'you simply weren't hitting the bomber with any of your shells!' Although he made several head-on attacks on heavy bomber formations, Pichler's aircraft was never once hit by an enemy bullet during any of them. This was in stark contrast to the attacks on the formations from the rear; he recalled one disastrous action when out of eight Messerschmitts in his *Staffel* two were shot down by the bombers and three, including his own, were forced to crash-land before they could even get into a firing position.

The American answer to the increasingly effective German fighter opposition was the provision of long-range escort fighters in large numbers. These aircraft, P-38 Lightnings, P-47 Thunderbolts and later P-51 Mustangs, were disposed above, in front and to the sides of selected bomber combat box formations, and could be summoned to the aid of other combat boxes in the vicinity which came under enemy fighter attack.

This move placed the German fighter pilots at a severe disadvantage. The heavy and unwieldy twin-engined Messerschmitt 110 and 410 bomber-destroyers suffered crippling losses and soon had to be withdrawn from action. The heavily armed German single-engined fighters also suffered severely and the Luftwaffe was forced to introduce the concept of separate 'heavy' and 'light' *Gruppen* of fighters. The Fw 190 bomber-destroyers retained their armour and their batteries of heavy cannon, and comprised the *Sturmgruppe* which was to engage the heavy bombers; simultaneously the 'light' *Gruppen*, equipped with lightly armed fighters with specially boosted engines, were to engage the bombers' escorts and prevent them from interfering. One *Sturmgruppe* and two covering *Begleitgruppen* comprised a *Gefechtsverband* (battle formation) with a strength of more than a hundred aircraft; it was the largest type of fighter formation ever to go into action under the leadership of one man, and also the least flexible.

When one of the mighty *Gefechtsverbaende* did connect with a bomber formation, the effect was usually devastating. The attack by one of these on July 7th 1944, led by Major Walther Dahl, accounted for most of the twenty-three B-24s lost by the U.S. 2nd Air Division that day. The American answer to the *Gefechtsverband* tactics was to mount large-scale fighter sweeps across the flanks of the bombers' route to catch and break up the unwieldy German formations before they could get close to their prey.

During the final nine months of the war the Germans employed their Me 163 and Me 262 jet fighters against the American bomber formations; these were fast enough to outrun the escorting Mustangs, and required no covering fighters except around their bases when they were flying slowly immediately after take-off and just before landing. When the jet fighters

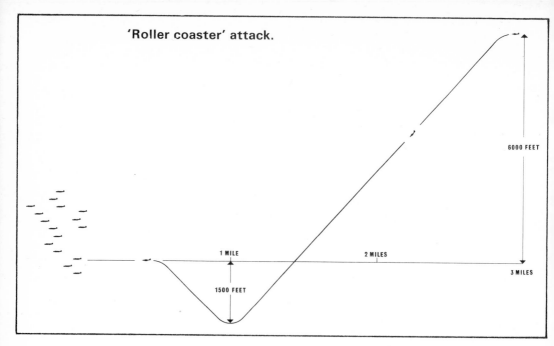

'Roller coaster' attack.

6000 FEET

1 MILE 2 MILES

3 MILES

1500 FEET

closed on the bombers, however, the very speed that had proved so useful for penetrating the screen of escorts became an embarrassment because it allowed only a very brief firing pass. To overcome this problem the German jet fighter pilots evolved a new type of attack. They dived through the screen of escorting fighters at speeds around 550 mph aiming for a point about 1 mile behind and about 1,500 feet beneath their quarry, then pulled up sharply to 'dump' speed before levelling off. At the end of this man-oeuvre the jet fighters were in an ideal position for the attack: they were inside the escorts, about 1,000 yards behind the bombers and with an overtaking speed of only about 100 mph. Because of its appearance to the bomber crews, this attack was known as the 'roller coaster' or the 'leap frog'.

Both the *Gefechtsverband* and the 'roller coaster' tactics were makeshift expedients, introduced because by mid-1944 the U.S. Army Air Force could put up far more fighters over Germany, most of them of higher quality and with better trained pilots, than those of the Luftwaffe. Once this state of affairs had been reached only a major technical improvement could swing back the scales. The Messerschmitt 262 in large numbers might have done this; but for a variety of reasons – due mainly to its radically different form of propulsion – this fighter was not available in quantity before the final chaos preceding the German collapse. Had sufficient Me 262s been available, the Luftwaffe would almost certainly have reverted to more conventional tactics for these fighters.

Opposite:

Meat in the 'Sandwich': a Messerschmitt 262 pictured closing in on a Mustang, while the latter's wing man (in the photographing aircraft) is himself closing in for the kill. *U.S.A.A.F.*

154

4 Summary.

It is right to be taught, even by an enemy.

OVID

In spite of the fears voiced in 1934, with radar-directed ground control the breed of fighter in service in 1939 had the performance to catch, and the fire-power to cleave down, the most modern bombers then operational. Once the war in the air began in earnest in the summer of 1940, the superiority of the fighter over the bombers in service was clearly demonstrated. Unescorted daylight bomber attacks became a rarity during the two years that followed, with the result that fighter-versus-fighter combat became much more important than had originally been envisaged. This in turn led to demands for increased performance, which were met by fitting more powerful – and therefore heavier – engines. At the same time there was a move to equip bombers and fighters with armour and self-sealing fuel tanks, which were weighty items themselves and which led to demands for heavier batteries of guns to defeat them. Range, too, assumed a new importance and fighters began to carry large internal and external loads of fuel. The effect of all of these moves was a considerable increase in the all-up weight of fighters, with a progressive reduction in manoeuvrability.

By the middle of 1942 the 20-mm cannon and heavy machine guns fitted to the British, American and Russian fighters were powerful enough to deal with the heaviest German and Japanese bombers; and they remained so for the rest of the war. For the Germans and the Japanese, however, the problem was rather different. The U.S. Army Air Force had never accepted as absolute the argument that the bomber could not stand up to the fighter. They had put a great deal of effort and money into building up a force of very heavily armed and armoured bombers to launch daylight precision bombing attacks on enemy industrial centres. While they were confronted by conventionally-armed fighters, the American heavy bombers proved that they could mount unescorted attacks without suffering heavy losses. The Germans learnt the lesson too, however, and under a crash programme began equipping their fighters with batteries of 30-mm and even 50-mm cannon, as well as air-to-air rockets, to defeat the raiders. During a series of hard-fought battles over Germany in the latter half of 1943, the fighter again proved that it could rule the skies. But to do so it had to carry such a weighty armament load that it became relatively slow and unwieldy; and when the Americans began sending long-range escort fighters with their bombers, the heavily armed bomber-destroyers

Opposite:
de Havilland Hornet.
C. Brown

157

fell as easy prey. In the skies over their homeland, the Japanese faced the fast, high-flying and formidably-armed B-29 Superfortress bomber; in spite of the most desperate measures, they never came close to defeating the American formations even when they came without escorts.

By 1944 fighter performance was nearing the physical limits imposed by the piston engine and the propeller. But by then the liquid-fuelled rocket and the turbo-jet engine were almost ready for service. The Germans won the race to get the new types of propulsion operational; but they had to cut too many corners to do so and ended up with a rocket motor that was just too exciting for general use, and a turbo-jet with a short running life. The British and American turbo-jets were better engineered and far more reliable, but the fighters they powered entered service too late to have any real effect.

Of the fighters in operational service at the end of the war the finest all-rounder was undoubtedly the German twin-jet Messerschmitt 262. Compared with the Spitfire I of 1939 it had nearly four times the engine thrust; its maximum speed of 540 mph and its rate of climb of 3,900 feet per minute were about one half greater and its weight of fire of 96 pounds fired in a three second burst was nearly ten times greater – and sufficient to cut down the most heavily armoured bomber. The two fighters had approximately the same wing area but the Me 262 was $2\frac{1}{2}$ times heavier, which meant that its wing loading and therefore its turning circle were greater by approximately the same amount. Had it been fitted with reliable jet engines such as those possessed by the Allies, and a properly working gyro gunsight, the Me 262 could have achieved great things. As it was, the German jet fighter's impact on the war was a matter of morale rather than a tangible physical effect.

On the question of tactics, at the beginning of the Second World War there was a divergence of opinion on what would be required from fighters; many air forces believed that their sole purpose would be to hunt down enemy bombers. Profiting from the lessons learnt during the Spanish Civil War, the Germans recognised that in any future conflict fighter-versus-fighter combat was not only possible but likely. The tactical doctrines expounded by the young Werner Moelders were found to give the best compromise between the conflicting requirements of fighter operations, and they gradually came to be adopted by all of the combatant air forces; with modifications, they have remained in use to the present day.

During the course of the Second World War fighters became faster, stronger and harder hitting. Yet no matter how good the machine was, its effectiveness in combat was not one jot greater than the combination of alertness, skill and aggressiveness of the man at the controls. There is much truth in the old adage:

> It isn't the size of the dog in the fight that counts,
> Its the size of the fight in the dog.

Select Bibliography

'Battle over the Reich' by Alfred Price, Ian Allan Ltd

'The Fighter Pilots' by Edward Sims, Cassel and Co Ltd

'Full Circle' by Air Vice Marshal J. Johnson, Chatto and Windus Ltd

'The Guns of the Royal Air Force 1939-1945' by G. F. Wallace, William Kimber Ltd

'Power to Fly' by L. J. K. Setright, Allen and Unwin Ltd

'Spitfire, the Story of a Famous Fighter' by Bruce Robertson, Harleyford Ltd

'Spitfire at War' by Alfred Price, Ian Allan Ltd

'War Planes of the Second World War', volumes 1, 2, 3 and 4, by William Green, Macdonald Ltd